No More Silence

No More Silence

How one woman's strength, courage & determination returned her voice

Debbie Widhalm

Cover credit, PeggyLee Hanson, Courageous Women Publications™

Debbie Widhalm

The Road Not Taken

https://RoadNotTaken.net

ISBN: 979-8-9922655-2-1

Warning–Disclaimer

This content contains sensitive themes that may be distressing or triggering for some individuals.

To my children and dear grandchildren,
I love you forever.

Table of Contents

Prologue

I have been asked why I wanted to write my life story. I have always been aware of an unseen hand guiding me throughout my life, even as a child.

I was born at a time when segregation was happening, and I never understood why my black friends were not loved as well as I was. It always bothered me to see them sad and not accepted in society. I was not taught that all are equal, but somehow, my heart knew they were.

As a child, my mother cleaned the house for a very rich woman. This lady had a girl my age who loved to play Barbies as much as I did. My mother would take me with her to play while she cleaned. I remember this little girl had apothecary jars full of Barbie shoes, purses, hats, and trinkets from the 60s that we played with. I was so enamored by her collection. I found myself throughout life walking through antique stores looking for jars like she had to collect trinkets so I could relive a time of privilege in my life.

I never paid attention to the color of skin, monetary worth, or popularity when I chose my friends. I had poor friends who I cared deeply for and kids I considered rich. I embraced my black friends and always loved all people from my heart.

I have walked through life accepting people right where they are, trying not to judge religions, differences, or skin colors. We are all people who want the same thing in life: love. Some of my dearest and best friends in life today are from Third World countries and other places. We are considered family, and pure acceptance is how our relationships started.

We live in a time where judgment rules people's hearts. Some are afraid to speak out because of this. It has become a very dangerous world. I believe that basic love and acceptance of all mankind is needed again.

I write my story to show you how I have stood up for what is right and found my voice when so many have silenced it. It is a journey of love, pain, loss, tragedy, death, and unimaginable grief. It is also a journey of miracles and guidance from an unseen force that never left my side.

I started life as a sixteen-year-old pregnant, uneducated, frightened young girl with little skills to navigate life alone. Somehow, that unseen hand protected and led me to safety countless times. I have seen angels; I have spoken to them, and I have experienced miracles that could have only come from above.

I hope you enjoy the journey you are about to take on how I made my choices in life and can realize that we are all here on this journey looking for love, peace, and acceptance.

We all matter, and we all have a voice. In time, I found my voice and have been set free from a lifetime of silence because I chose to do unpopular things, stand up for myself, and speak out. It was never easy and quite often very lonely, but today, I am free and looking forward to the next chapter.

~ Debbie Widhalm

Acknowledgments

I would like to thank Tammy Kling for noticing me in the fall of 2023. I consider you my friend and have loved our conversations and your expert help.

Thank you, PeggyLee Hanson, for all your education and expert guidance this year. You are dear to my soul; I consider you a dear friend, and I am endowed to you for helping me bring this book to fruition. I look forward to continuing our journey.

Thank you, Cate Raphael, for telling me in 2019, it was time to release all the books I carry in my heart! I treasure your friendship with gratitude.

Thank you to all my children and grandchildren who have made my life much richer; life without you would not be worthwhile. I love you all deeply forever.

Thank you, my Sana, Zu, Sara, Ayyad, Zaiden, Mustafa, Mauz, and Solomon, all of whom are my beloved family sent directly from Heaven. I love you all dearly forever.

Zaiden, Ayyad, Mustafa, and dear Mauz, God made me your grandma at a time when my grandma's heart was broken into a million pieces. I love you deeply. Thank you for choosing me.

I want to thank God for the birth of my dear firstborn. We traveled life together for a long time in deep love, had many laughs, and shared a great life together. You are part of my soul, and I treasure and love you forever.

Thank you to my second-born child, who is wise and willing to extend forgiveness. We have grown a lot, and I love you deeply forever.

Thank you, Randy, Kelly, Michele, Hannah, and Vincent, for enriching my life. I am grateful for the love we share; I love you all dearly.

I want to express deep love to my mother, who did her very best to navigate life's waters. You came from a place of deep abuse, and I hope for you to heal from all the trauma. I speak of our trials in this book, but you are the strength of our family, the chord we all have a common hold to. I love you deeply and hold nothing but gratitude and love in my heart for all your efforts, sacrifices, and attempts. You Matter, too!

Thank you to God for choosing me to walk this journey through all its ups and downs while sending angels in human form time after time to encourage me. You never left me alone.

Finally, thank you, Dean, for being teachable and willing to put the hard work in to make a life together work in love. We have overcome the impossible. Our faith in each other and God has been the necessary constant. I love you forever.

Chapter 1

It was a scorching hot Saturday morning in Moore, Oklahoma, in early August, when my mother asked me if I was pregnant. I had just completed the eleventh grade and was seventeen years old.

After cleaning the bathroom with Pine Sol, I just gave the final rinse. The window was open, and a gentle breeze circulated the strong but clean smell in the air.

I looked up to see my mother enter the room with a serious look on her face. She closed the door, which sent shivers down my spine. I suddenly felt a bit nauseous and wanted to run, but I knew it was time to face the truth.

She said she had noticed I had not been needing pads for my period. Then, the long, dreaded question came. “Debra, are you pregnant?”

I hung my head in shame. “I think so,” I fearfully said.

With disappointment in her eyes, she said, “We need to get you to a doctor then.” She left almost as quickly as she had entered.

I was stunned, embarrassed, ashamed, petrified, and left alone in my feelings. I had carried this day in my heart for months. Now my mother knew, and I had to face the reality that I was carrying another soul inside me.

Even though she didn’t say much, I was relieved she had asked.

I stood in the bathroom doorway for a long time, scared to walk out. I felt like I had committed an unforgivable sin and that my siblings would judge and hate me. Finally, I gently opened the door so it wouldn’t make any noise. I quietly crept into my bedroom, closed the door, and stayed there until evening.

The doctor’s appointment was the next day. He confirmed I was a few days away from entering my fifth month. I was given the option of aborting the baby. As I sat on the table, my mother reminded me of how young I was and that my life was just beginning. She said life would drastically change if I kept the baby, and my career options would be limited. It seemed she and the doctor thought it would be a good decision for me long term to abort, but we would need to do it soon.

I didn't realize that the small fluttering I had been feeling and seeing in my belly was the baby's movement. Until I had this knowledge, I had just been pretending that none of this was real. I kept looking each day for my period.

When I realized the baby was real and alive, I made a choice. As terrified as I was about becoming a mother, I could not kill this child!

I turned seventeen in June, so I was still very much an adolescent. I hadn't even thought of leaving home anytime soon. Somehow, the courage to follow my gut responded, and I found my voice, "No, I'll keep him," I said.

No one tried to change my mind and accepted my decision.

My younger brother had driven us to the doctor that day and was in the waiting room. He, my mother, and I went back to our house in complete silence.

I didn't know what having a conversation looked like with my mother about emotional issues, so I didn't miss the support. All I felt was that I had done this to myself because of a poor decision, and I had to pay for my mistake.

I remember thinking in the car ride home about having a baby and never being able to date anyone else. I thought how much it would hurt to get the child out of me. I was sure I would deserve the pain of getting pregnant as a teenager.

My thoughts were scattered and sometimes dark.

I would have to support a child now and be called mommy. I hadn't finished high school and didn't want to go back to face the judgment and name-calling.

My school was small, with grades seven through twelve in one building. The average grade contained about twenty students, and sometimes, there were less than that. Everyone knew everyone's business, and my pregnancy was a hot topic.

I had often thought I would travel the world as an airline stewardess. I couldn't see that happening now.

I considered opening the door and jumping out.

My brother must have read my mind as he gently reached back and locked my door.

He was quietly watching me. There were moments I would look up in the rearview mirror and catch him gazing at me with deep compassion in his eyes. He never said anything, but those looks gave me strength.

There was never a great rapport between my siblings, my mother, and me. We just all shared a house, biding our time in life. It was understood that we loved each other, but none of us were close.

My sister and I were three years apart, and I was the older one. We played dolls together when we were younger and shared a room, but she was always quiet and introspective. I always felt my mother favored her over me.

As we became teenagers, she would say how pretty my sister was and what a perfect body she had, and she would say how I looked better with makeup on, which made me feel I was not naturally pretty like my sister. My older brother often said the same thing to me, and I grew up feeling so ugly and inadequate.

I remember being at my grandparents' house as a teenager, and someone said how beautiful my mother's daughters were to her. Her response was, "Yes, my youngest is gorgeous."

My grandmother interjected, "Well, so is Debbie!"

"Yeah, but not like her sister. She's va-va-va voom!"

Many relatives had heard the exchange. At that moment, I hung my head in embarrassment. That stuck with me, and I internalized it for years. I knew I would never look or be good enough for my mother.

My sister and I were both slender and gifted with naturally full breasts. Mine seemed to grow overnight. I remember waking up one day and putting on a shirt that wasn't loose for school. I noticed how big my breasts had grown. They were huge! Some friends asked me if they were real or if it was toilet paper! I was embarrassed but proud that I had grown such perky ones.

My friends always said I was pretty, but my mother's voice was always louder.

We don't realize how we program our children to become an image that makes us look successful until the damage is done. When children are not given a choice, how can they learn to trust their ability to choose later? It can set them up for being bullied because they are not confident enough in their own skin to show up for themselves.

We all need to be able to lean into the voice that guides us as we grow. When we take someone's voice away, we control another human and do not allow their natural gifts to develop as they were meant to.

While our job as a parent is to guide and teach our children, controlling their choices quiets their voice to speak up. Over time, they give up speaking because they know they are only here to please their parents, and it doesn't matter what they think. This is also how I grew up.

I once witnessed a three-year-old child say, "It doesn't matter. Ask mommy," when asked which dress she liked the best. She had already figured out that her desires didn't matter. She figured out that she had no control over her choices in life very early. She learned to say it doesn't matter and grew up that way. She was bullied in school as fear crippled her voice.

My younger brother always seemed favored. He was always extra close to both my parents, and it appeared they would automatically take his word or side in any disagreement or problem throughout life. I never understood how they got as close to him as they did. It created jealousy and distance between us.

He was a loner and must have had his own struggles none of us knew about. For years, my siblings and I called him the "pet." I remember how quiet and sad he would get when he heard us. I don't know what he went through, but the nickname seemed to hurt his feelings. Maybe he didn't feel as loved as we thought he was.

My dad and my older brother fought a lot when he was in school and throughout life. He never seemed to get the same love and grace my younger brother got, and I would see him cry when he was alone. He struggled and was always alone at school, too. I wanted to cry when I saw him looking sad and alone on our breaks from class.

During his last year at home, he and my dad would fist-fight each other. It was a sight that broke my heart, and I never understood it. My heart always went out to him, and I would pray for him that God would heal his broken heart.

At seventeen, he left home, married, and joined the United States Army. He finished his senior year in Colorado, where he was stationed. He had a very successful and decorated career serving with the elite. I've always been proud that he found a way to shine in life with his talents despite all the sadness.

My younger sister got married in the mid-1980s, and everyone in the family came to the wedding. She and her husband-to-be were in med school to become doctors. It was a big affair, and all the relatives were impressed with the two doctors in the family.

After the wedding, my grandmother and older brother talked, and he asked her if she knew why he was always treated differently. She told him because my father adopted him. When he and my mother got married, my brother was three. He was her first husband's biological son. My mother told me this one night after I became pregnant. It didn't matter to me that he was adopted. He was my brother, and it changed nothing for me. But he was almost thirty years old when she told him. He blew his top that my parents had kept this a secret from him all these years.

When he found out, my mother blamed me for telling him. She never believed that it wasn't me. As it turned out, my cousins, aunts, and uncles all knew. Everyone in the family knew except my brother! They had all kept the secret. That's a lot of control!

I was always the one who noticed everything in life. I hated lies and never understood the purpose of dark family secrets. I believed in living the truth. If there was injustice, I would do everything in my power to help heal it. I always tried to be a bridge and carried a deep empathy toward others that, at times, was more than I could handle. My shoulders were huge, and everyone cried on them.

My mother and father accused me of breaking up our family home after my grandmother told my brother about his being adopted. There was nothing I could do to convince them that I didn't do it!

I always carried my three siblings deep in my heart and prayed to God that he would always keep and protect them.

Chapter 2

We were religious and attended the Assembly of God church growing up. My mother was active as a youth director and made our gatherings fun. I remember her teaching us the songs "Amen" and "Soon and Very Soon" by Andre Crouch. The songs were lively and full of spirit!

Once, she arranged for us to go to a church only the black community attended, where we performed these two songs and got involved as everyone clapped and danced to God. Being united in God with friends, our group—usually shunned—felt so good. It felt right—we were all worshiping the same God who knew each of us by name. That service is one of my favorite childhood memories.

That day, in my heart, I decided to always love every human on purpose, and that decision stuck with me for the rest of my life. It hurt me to think that my new friends were judged just because their skin was darker than mine. Our skin color, culture, or religion did not make God love us any more or any less. He knew the count of every hair on our heads!

My mother was in college at the time, in the mid to late 1960s, and it was her way of bringing to light what she was learning—that all are created equal in God's eyes.

She was so very good with others, but her deep, injured child had trouble giving equally to her own children. There were things she said and did to me that I vowed never to embrace and repeat.

I took note of her professional choices, though. How she treated and led others were profound and excellent examples of how I wanted to be seen. I chose from those experiences what I would keep in the inventory of my life choices. She was an excellent mother, given the skills she had to work with from her upbringing.

My grandmother would come each May and pick me up, and we would go to Paris, Texas, until August. I had done this since I was eight years old.

I had four cousins who lived there, one of whom was the same age as me. We all grew up together, having innocent make-believe fun until I was fifteen years old. That was my last summer in Paris.

I met a guy I talked to as a friend all summer while working at my aunt's burger shop. It was a good, healthy friendship with a boy who I had no romantic interest in. We laughed at farts, ate burgers, and listened to music at the burger joint all summer. He called me Cher because my hair was long, straight, and black. He said I was beautiful, and it made me feel good.

He was there when my parents picked me up for the summer. I introduced him to them and told them he wanted to come visit me sometime in Oklahoma. On the ride home, they forbade me from ever talking to him again, calling him a hippie. He had long hair and drove an El Camino, and they didn't want me to be around any "damn hippies."

They didn't believe me when I told them he was a really nice guy and I wasn't interested in him as a boyfriend. I really wasn't; he was just a guy and a good, funny friend, which was good for me at the time.

It was happening again—not being able to make my own choices.

This was the second time they had made a choice for my future by not trusting me enough to follow my own intuition. I had to put another good friend on the list of forbidden people in my life.

It happened the first time when I was in the fourth grade and befriended a beautiful black girl named Verdelmar. We fell in love as friends and loved to play together at recess. I didn't care that she wasn't the same as me.

We enjoyed so many of the same foods and laughed all day together. I loved her differences. I felt she was just like me, and I accepted her without preconceived concepts that others had.

I was punished with a spanking and forbidden to talk to her after my parents found out about our friendship. It broke my heart and soul. I was programmed that I didn't have the ability or wisdom to make my own life choices and not to trust my gut.

The third time this happened, I was a freshman in high school. I had been crushing on a boy since seventh grade. He was the only boy I would have chosen to date if I could decide. He was very handsome with striking blue eyes. I could have fallen in love with him and would say I did, from afar. I was so happy when he asked me out, and my parents let me go.

After he picked me up, he drove to a dirt road by my house. I could see he wanted to kiss me, and I wanted him to. I had been waiting a long time for him.

While driving, he stared at me and ran off into a ditch. He was stuck and couldn't get out. He walked to the neighbor's house to call his dad and told me I would have to walk home. It wasn't far. The neighbor saw me and phoned my parents, who were waiting for me when I arrived. They asked me where he was, and I told them what had happened.

I never got my kiss and was spanked and told never to speak to him again. I was warned that if anyone saw me talking to him, my dad would come to school and spank me in front of everyone. I had shunned another one of my choices in life and added his name to the list.

I gave up after that and kept my head down. I had been conditioned that my voice didn't count and I was too young to make decisions of the heart.

There was a lot of jealousy between my siblings and me; it was always about my mother. She had gone back to school when I was a young elementary student and worked hard to get her master's degree in special education.

My mother became a schoolteacher, and I was always jealous of her students. They seemed to get the side of her I wanted and never saw. She openly loved them and was a powerful and influential teacher.

Had she been able to give me the kind of love I watched her give them, life may have been different. I realize she did her best, and I know she loved me the best she knew how.

My mother was a trailblazer in her time and was very successful professionally. I have always been proud of her tenacity to follow her dream and take her inner child out of the poverty mindset she grew up in. She was the only one of her six siblings who went to college, and she was proud of that.

She came from an alcoholic father who had sex with his daughters and beat my grandmother. Very little food was around, and they lived in a shack in the Panhandle of Texas. One of her sibling sisters tried to drown her over jealousy of a boy.

My mother was made fun of for being poor, smelly, and having only one dress. Her childhood wounds never left her, and the neglect she experienced from her own parents was horrendous.

The abuse my mother grew up in was unending. Her parents wanted her out of the house after they found out she was pregnant at the age of fifteen. Mom ran into the arms of him, the same boy her sister tried to drown her over.

She was a survivor, and life seemed very cruel to her until she met my father. He was her savior and brought her out of an abusive life. He was her protector and never faltered from that job. He met and married her when she was nineteen.

I can't blame my mother for not knowing how to show unconditional love to me because she didn't know it existed until she met my dad. It did damage me, though. Growing up, I never felt very close to my mom, and I often felt judged by her. I had little respect for her because I saw her love others the way she couldn't love me. I grew up resenting her for this.

My father took over the parental roles while she went to school full-time for years and then went to work. He was very strict, but I knew he loved me. He was always there for me when it counted. I always remember him being the one to comfort me when I was scared or had a problem.

My dad was a good man and came from a more stable home. He had a terrible temper and believed in spankings, but he had a heart of gold. He would help anyone he could.

My sister and I took over the housework and cooking at a very young age. I didn't mind because cleaning my mom's house gave me an outlet for all my frustrations in life. I always loved to rearrange furniture and did so almost every day.

I would get in trouble for moving things around so much, but it met a strong and vital need in me, and I loved how beautiful and clean it made things look. As it turned out, rearranging furniture became my outlet for dealing with life. My house always looked clean, and people were amazed at how I could come up with so many ways to make a room look different.

Chapter 3

The car ride home after my initial doctor's visit stirred up many thoughts and memories of how I had gotten to this point in my life. My brother had brought us safely back home, and I went into my room, where I had dozed off when the familiar sound of the garage door opening woke me up.

My father came home at 5:00 p.m. that day. I was so scared to see him and sat in complete fear. I expected to get yelled at or slapped. I sat up on the side of my bed and knew he would be in to talk to me soon.

As he opened my door, I froze. I was shaking and shocked when he came into the room and gave me a big, silent hug. I began to cry and apologize to him for getting pregnant. He softly comforted me, saying, "Don't worry, baby, we will get through this; it's going to be alright."

His reaction shocked me, but I knew he would help me, and somehow, it would all work out. I deeply respected his love and support and felt loved by him.

It was now time to tell Billy, the father of my baby, that I was pregnant.

We began dating after he came to our house with my older brother and saw me. I caught him looking at me, and the next day, he called me to ask me out. I really wasn't that attracted to him, but I agreed to go. My parents were all for it and encouraged me to go out with him.

He and I had been dating for several months. I wasn't in love with him and never saw myself with him forever. He was a nice guy with a beautiful smile. He was very polite to my parents and communicated well, which impressed them. We went to an occasional movie and rode his horse a lot, but we mostly made out on the dirt roads nearby.

He was a couple of years older than I was and was scared to death when I told him about the baby. After he told his mom and dad, the two families met at his house to discuss marriage.

I could tell by the way his mother and sisters glared at me that they didn't like me.

The meeting was quick and to the point. There was no idle talk and no lingering afterward. Billy's father immediately took charge, looked me in the eyes, and said, "Young lady, do you love my boy?"

I was terrified of his voice, tone, the look in his eyes, and the protective way he said, "... do you love my boy?" I also noted that he chose not to call me by name, thus intimidating me, which I felt was intentional. Yet, I felt I had no choice but to say yes to his question.

The truth could not be spoken at this time. "No sir, I'm sorry, I don't love your boy. I liked him as a boyfriend, but I was not in love with him," which is what I wanted to say. I knew very little about him. We never talked about dreams, religion, culture, or family history; we just made out a lot.

I don't even remember if I knew his birthday. I knew he was a good baseball player, and he was a cowboy and wanted to be an auctioneer; he was an alcoholic at age nineteen, and he loved his parents and sisters very much.

Everyone decided we needed to get married as soon as possible since I would deliver the baby in four months. We married a few days later at the Justice of the Peace with all siblings and our parents present.

As a gift from one of his friends, we were given a beautiful cabin surrounded by trees deep in the woods. It had a screened-in porch and a wooden pathway that led from the cabin to a big pond out in the country in Seminole, Oklahoma. It was a beautifully serene setting. Had I not been so scared and alone, I would have enjoyed it to the fullest.

We could live there for one year rent-free. It was fully furnished, and we had to take a trailer of horses to Red River, New Mexico, for the owner. We stayed a few days in Red River, which was our honeymoon. It was a beautiful place in the mountains. We rode motor scooters around town. We enjoyed laughing with each other, and I was surprised at how much fun we had.

It was hard to sleep with another person. Even though we had previously had sex, we'd never been in bed together. We had never completely gone all the way, and it hurt a lot when we finally did. I remembered hearing the doctor tell my mother that my hymen was still unbroken. I didn't know then what that meant and forgot to ask, so it was never mentioned again. Obviously, it was enough to get those swimmers in contact with my eggs!

I was very disappointed with the whole sex thing, probably because the mystery and fantasy were gone. There was no romance, and we were both scared of the unknown and felt pressured to marry each other.

I was homesick for my parents and siblings and wished I'd not married. I was not happy. All I could see was a long and boring journey for the rest of my life. I lived in deep regret and was very sad.

As we left Red River, New Mexico, early one August morning, with the radio on and windows down, "Touch Me in the Morning," by Diana Ross, came on. I was a Soul Town fan and turned up the volume.

I became sad at the thought that he would be the one with me in the morning from now on. I realized I couldn't listen to my favorite music anymore, fantasizing about my dream guy. We didn't even listen to the same music. He was all country, and I was all soul!

I felt trapped with someone I didn't want to be with and saw no way out.

We drove straight to his parents' house from Red River in time for dinner. I was not comfortable around his sisters and parents because they focused all their attention on him and gave me dirty looks.

I was hungry but ate tiny portions that night and pretended to be full. I did not want to make them any angrier at me than I felt they already were. I could feel their glares, so I kept my eyes down most of the time around them. I was very quiet and spoke only when spoken to, which was very little.

They could probably tell we weren't happy or meant to be together. Honestly, I was always scared when I was near them. I could feel hatred from their body language.

I could see that Billy was relieved to see his parents, and I longed to see mine. Neither of us was ready for this change in our relationship.

As we drove to our new home that night, I got a glimpse of my future and had never felt lonelier. I realized it was a long way out of town, and we had no phone. I noticed that I was only about a mile from one of my best friends in high school. At least I would be able to walk to her sometimes to talk.

Chapter 4

Billy got up early the following day, fed his parents' animals, and then worked at the feed store, which became his routine.

I spent all of my time alone, sweeping and mopping every day. I would rearrange furniture constantly for something to do. I loved to decorate and had been used to cleaning my mom's house, so I was thankful for lots of options and floor space to work with.

When I moved a piece of furniture, I seemed to feel something shift inside me. I learned to manage my feelings this way. Since there was no one to talk to, God gave me this effective source to channel my thoughts, frustrations, fears, and worries about my future.

I also talked to him a lot. I felt he was out in the country with me and my unborn child and was protecting us with invisible forces. I had always believed in His angels, and my gut told me I needed them now.

My husband would stop and eat at his parents' house most days after the feed store; I don't remember eating much. Surely, he must have brought me food sometimes when he ate, but my memory is dim. I do know there was no food in the house on a regular basis.

My friend worked at Safeway and told me to come in. She would give us a big bill of groceries for five dollars, ring things up for a penny and a nickel, and before long, we had a lot of food to take home. I guess that's how I fed myself when I was there. I often went home to my parents for a couple of weeks, and they ensured I ate well then.

We were married for eight months, but I was only at the cabin for maybe three months collectively.

My best friend would take me to my parents when Billy got mean. This always made him and his parents mad. Eventually, the real feelings of his mother and siblings began to surface.

They hated me and began to show it by calling me names. They would start fights with me and threaten to beat me up. They called me whore and bitch and said I took their brother and son from them.

I was with Billy one day when he stopped at his parents' house.

When I got out of the truck, his mother said," What is she doing here?"

He said, "Mom, we won't be here long."

She said, "You are always welcome, son, but I don't want this whore on my property!"

I screamed, "I'm not a whore!"

His four sisters and mother came at me, got in my face, pushed me, and called me a "slutty whore bitch." They warned me that they would be taking my child from me the instant it was born. I couldn't believe they were treating me this way, and I had to stand alone because my husband always took their side. These people were not interested in embracing me and were out to destroy me.

That gut feeling I had been getting was beginning to make sense. One thing they didn't count on, though, were the angels God had dispatched to my side!

I really wasn't a whore or a slut. He was my first boyfriend, first kiss, first everything. I was from a good family. I was a kind girl with a heart filled with love for people, and I said my prayers every day.

I had a lot of friends and always talked to everyone. It was not my nature to shun anyone. I liked spending time with my girlfriends listening to music. I played high school basketball and never got into trouble. I didn't drink, nor was I ever drawn to drugs or smoking.

Life was pretty naïve for me up until now.

Chapter 5

Since marrying Billy, my prayers have never ceased. I lived in fear of being hurt and prayed every day for God's divine protection upon my life.

Something inside me began to grow, and I became more determined than ever to take the best care of this baby. I would protect him from these vicious people, and they would have to kill me first to steal my baby, as they began to threaten this more frequently.

These people hated me and were determined to hurt me, make me miscarry, physically take my child, or kill me. These are things they told me, and I believed them! Little did I know, I was at the beginning of a battle that only God could help me fight and win!

Billy worked at an auction house once a week in Oklahoma City, Oklahoma, and I stayed with my parents. Sometimes, I would stay an extra week, and he would pick me up on his way back.

My parents moved to Moore, Oklahoma, in June early in the 1970s. It was about fifty miles away from Seminole, where we were living.

I felt very unsafe being so far away from them and not having a phone. Sometimes, I would walk to my friend's house through the pasture and use her phone to contact my parents if I needed them. We would make plans for a rendezvous on a particular day.

On one of my visits with my parents, I remember my mother telling me how she woke up one night thinking about me. She was terrified for my life and prayed for God to protect me and dispatch angels to my side. I never forgot how it made me feel to hear my mother pray for me in the middle of the night and ask God to send me help! I felt so loved by her and much safer after that.

As I got closer to my due date, my parents helped us get a phone in the cabin. God forbid I would be alone so far from help and go into labor. It was a good move.

The truck wouldn't start one day, so Billy had to borrow his parents' truck. I was tired of being alone for so long, so he let me keep the truck for the day. I drove him to work and planned to pick him up afterward. I hadn't been home long after dropping him off when I saw his mother speeding into our driveway.

She slammed her car door and screamed, "You damned slutty bitch, give me my damn keys. How dare you drive my truck! I'm going to hurt you!"

I locked the screen door, and she ripped right through it!

I grabbed the keys as she stormed through my living room. In a horrendous rage, she grabbed my long black hair and pulled me backward, falling on the floor. She hit me in the stomach, and I kicked at her and got her off of me.

Still on the floor, she saw the keys in one of my hands and stomped on my hand, over and over again; she stomped my hand until it began to bleed! She may have gotten scared when she saw the blood.

She threw me across the room and, in her vilest voice, warned me, "This will not end until we take that baby from you, you nasty slutty whore!!!"

I screamed, "Try! You will NEVER get my son, NEVER!"

As she drove away that morning, I knew our life was in danger, and the anger only grew between his family and me.

I fell on my knees and raised my arms to the only one who could help me. I cried for hours to God to never let them take my child or hurt me. Please send your angels down to protect us, I begged.

The mother instinct had taken over, and I would never back down to these people. My strength came from God! Thank God my parents had taught me to pray. It was my only weapon.

My parents got tired of hearing about them calling me names and trying to fight me. One day, my parents, brothers, sister, and his parents, along with his sisters, all decided to settle this feud once and for all. Everyone met at our cabin with fists swinging. Each person had paired up and was hitting someone when the police showed up. The police hauled all of us downtown to the police station.

My husband's family was trying to press charges on my brother for a cut on their daughter's eye. But I caused the cut by hitting her with my class ring! I felt a little proud that day that I caused her some of the pain she had been throwing my way. They couldn't press charges on me because I was a minor.

I didn't realize how much anger was building up inside me because of this family's daily abuse. It would take many years to identify the anger I had to bury over all this—anger that came out when I was triggered by fear.

My dad and I were looking out the window when a policeman came to us and said, "You know, one of these days, you guys are going to be able to look back on this day and laugh about it."

I remember hearing my dad say, "I sure hope so."

It had been so long since I had laughed or smiled. I longed for that emotion just to come and rescue me! My life felt dark and hopeless as I lived in constant fear.

I can look back now and see it as a Hatfield and McCoy moment; it is funny but still very scary. They were violent people.

I remember my feelings well. I often found myself on my knees alone in that cabin, crying out in prayer. "God," I said, "these people want to hurt me, and I am the only person here to protect myself and my child."

As the tears flowed, I begged God to send his legions of angels to protect me and my little baby. I remember hearing people talk about angels showing up in legions before, and I knew it would take many to rescue us. I promised Him I would be the best mother I could be and give my child the best life possible.

Chapter 6

I had reached my ninth month, and the threats continued to come by telephone and through my husband from his family. The hate for me was very real. They knew I would never relinquish my child, and they were as determined as ever to hurt me. They had convinced my husband to take my child.

Billy and I were having a good day together and went to the high school basketball game. I had been having low back pain for about eight hours, and it kept getting more intense.

I started hurting so badly at the game that I couldn't stand it. Billy called his mother, and she said, "It sounds like she has been in labor for a while; you better go to the hospital."

We were less than an hour from the hospital in Oklahoma City, Oklahoma. Billy and one of his good friends made the drive together. By the time we got there, I was about an hour away from meeting my precious son, whom I had already fought so hard for.

The sister came in to shave and prep me for delivery, and with a stern and judgmental frown, she asked, "How old are you?"

I said I was seventeen as I hung my head in humiliation. I was very embarrassed and felt like she thought I was all the names I had been called the past few months. How would I ever be able to prove to people that I was not a slut. That name made me feel like the most unlovable human alive.

She didn't say much to me after that, except that she would be giving me an enema. I got the enema and barely made it into the bathroom before I shot poop all over the bathroom wall! As if I couldn't be more humiliated, she screamed at me when she walked in and saw me on the floor cleaning poop while in active labor. Sister demanded I get back in bed and scolded me for being so stupid! I apologized and climbed back in bed.

A short time later, they wheeled me into the delivery room alone. I remember the pain being so bad I kept rubbing my stomach. The mean nun who had yelled at me before told me to get my hands off my stomach. The way she glared and yelled at me made me feel like I had done something nasty and had violated her eyes!

I was so ashamed. I couldn't help it; I kept instinctively rubbing my stomach, so she strapped my arms down with restraints. I felt like a prisoner as I obeyed each command to push my son out of my body with my arms strapped down on the bed.

I had to catalog another violent act against me.

I buried the fear, shock, and traumatic behavior deep under the feelings that had already begun to gather in my soul. I saw my soul as a huge jar with a lid. Each time someone hurt me, I pushed that feeling into my soul jar and screwed the lid on tightly. I did not have the skills to know how to handle these feelings. I had to protect myself to survive. Getting rid of the pain by burying it seemed to help at the time.

It seemed I was being punished by a lot of judging people who didn't appreciate me getting pregnant so young, and none of them were shy about letting me know. I got the memo loud and clear; everyone thought I was a slut!

I remained courageous; it was all I had.

Another soul was depending on me now. I would have to figure this feeling out later on in life.

Somehow, my courage and power were not of this world. I had learned to tap into a power that would guide me for the rest of my life.

I remember attending church one night when I was about twelve. One of my dear friends and I had prayed at the altar for hours on a Sunday night. People kept trying to get us to stop, but we were so deep in prayer we couldn't. It felt like I had left this world.

I sat with God for hours. It was magical and empowering. I can see now that He was preparing me for a battle a few years down the road by giving me strength and faith. It wouldn't be hard to call on Him because I knew Him well, and His power was only a request away.

After I delivered my son, I saw Billy once in the four days I was in the hospital. I named the baby myself, which made him mad. He wanted him called Junior and named after him. There was no way I was going to do that. I got to pick the name, which I found while reading a book as I convalesce in the hospital.

He picked me up and took me home to Seminole the evening I was discharged. My parents had taken a trip and were out of town during my baby's delivery and hospital stay.

It was a lonely time.

When we got to Seminole, he drove to his parents' house to get his sister.

I asked him why she was coming over. He said, "To take care of little Junior."

I said, "No, she isn't. I will be taking care of my own baby."

He brought her anyway, against my wishes. When we got into the house, he told me to give the baby to his sister.

"No!" I said.

I had taken him upstairs to the bedroom and had him in my arms. He yelled for his sister to come upstairs and help him get the baby so he could give it to their mom. His sister was a big girl, and I wasn't, and I was bleeding very heavily after my delivery. I was passing clots the size of baseballs. The doctor said it was normal and to just take it easy.

Billy threw me on the bed and pinned me down. I had my baby in my left arm, holding him with all my might. He was on top of me, trying to get the baby out of my left arm while his sister sat on the other arm.

They both cussed and yelled and slapped me and tried again and again to pull the child from my arms. He finally slapped me across the face, called me horrible names, and gave up.

After they sped away in a rage, I held my son tightly, comforted him as best I could, and thanked God for his miraculous help! There was no other explanation except that God was in the room with me and didn't want my child to be taken away.

I called my mother the next morning, told her what had happened, and they came to get me. We spent time with them recovering and getting used to not living in fear.

My husband always talked me into coming back each time I left. Nothing ever changed; it only got worse.

Chapter 7

One hot spring day in April, Billy got up and said he was tired of me and I needed to get my ass out of his life. He began to throw all my clothes and purse out in the front yard. After everything I owned, which wasn't much, was thrown out, he called his parents.

I heard him say, "Today, we are taking Junior from this bitch. Get the guns off the back porch."

He told them he was leaving now to come and bring them back. The moment he drove away, I ran to the phone and called my parents in desperation and fear.

My dad answered the phone almost immediately.

I said, "Daddy, I can't talk, but I need you now! Billy and his parents are bringing guns to kill me. I am leaving now. Pick me up at Sheila's house! He said, "Be careful, honey. I'll be there in forty-five minutes."

I had to get out of there fast because they would be in a rush to get back to me. My son was wearing a white T-shirt and a diaper. I had just made him a bottle and grabbed it. I noticed all I owned on the ground as I tripped past it and ran for my life!

It was about a mile across the pasture to my friend's house. As I ran, I saw a truck coming, it was them! I threw myself on the ground and began to crawl like a soldier on my stomach. I did this until I reached my friend's house.

I remember looking down at my baby and seeing his eyes round and big as he felt my fear! My heart melted. I begged for rescue and promised I'd do whatever God asked of me and always be a good mother to this precious soul.

Thankfully, I made it unseen to my friend's house and knocked on their door. I knocked several times, and no one answered. As I panicked, I looked all around the outside and noticed a wash house. I tried to open the door, and it was padlocked! I ran around to the back and saw a window. I tried to open it, and it worked! I climbed into the shed and closed the window.

I made a bed with fresh sheets from the dryer. There was just enough space between the washer and dryer to cradle my son. Thank God he felt safe and never cried.

In the meantime, I could hear Billy and his family yelling, "Bitch, where are you?" Then, I would hear them fire a gun into the air.

I was terrified!

The window I had climbed into was facing our property. I could see their forms as they looked into the barn and all around the house for me. I locked the window, in case they thought to come to my friend's house.

Dad had called the sheriff to warn him of the situation. The sheriff met him there.

It was the longest forty-five minutes of my life. There was a hole big enough in the wall to see when cars were coming from the direction my dad would be coming from. I went back and forth, watching for my dad and those who wanted to harm me! Thankfully, my baby slept through the wait in the shed.

I jumped every time I heard them fire the gun in the air. They weren't giving up.

Dad arrived as fast as he could drive. I saw his car through the peephole, grabbed my son, climbed out of the window, and ran to get into it. My uncle was with him, and I gave my son to him.

I said, "Daddy, we have to get out of here as fast as possible. They've been shooting guns!"

As he sped out of the driveway, the sheriff and Billy's parents met us on the road. His sister jumped out of their truck, ran towards me, and grabbed my hair through the rolled-down window. We had no air conditioning in the car. She began to hit me in the head while screaming obscenities at me! I tried to roll the window up as my dad accelerated.

Billy's sister finally had to let go.

They followed us halfway back to Moore, Oklahoma, shooting us the finger while behind us. At least it wasn't the gun I had heard being shot earlier, the one intended for me.

Chapter 8

It would remain etched in my memory forever how God showed up and saved us again. I thanked Him for the miraculous rescue and for everything working smoothly when I needed it to. He was protecting us as a new family, and I owed him my life.

We made it back home. I promised my dad I would never go back. He said we'd get a lawyer and get rid of these people once and for all. I was so thankful my parents loved me and wanted to help us! I had a home with them until I could support my son on my own. They would help us get to the next stage in life.

I kept my promise to God to do whatever He told me to. I began to go to church religiously. I prayed at least two hours a day in my closet and started reading the Bible. It soon became my favorite book, and I was never without it.

I was kneeling in prayer one day when I saw myself in a white uniform attending to people. I felt God asking me to become a nurse.

As I mentioned earlier, I completed the eleventh grade and had no driver's license. I went to the nearest Junior college, took the GED test, passed, and got my license.

I enrolled in Nurse's Aide training and got a job at the hospital where I delivered my son. I worked for the next three years, taking care of people's bodies and souls. I had completely devoted my life to God and became His missionary.

My life was spent in prayer, reading the Bible, going to church with my son, and talking and praying with my patients every day.

I had forgotten about the soul jar and didn't need to deposit any new feelings in it for a while.

A preacher had told me the quickest way to heal was to serve others. He said, "If you look at ways to make someone else's life better, you aren't focusing on your own problems, and that diminishes the power over you."

So, that's what I chose to do. I chose to live for others and make everyone in my pathway as happy and comfortable as I could.

I was amazed at how God led me to people right in the nick of time. I prayed with many people and held their hands as they took their last breaths. I had told Jesus that I would be his wife until further notice. I walked with God and had great peace in my life. It felt so good to be safe!

My dad had gotten a lawyer, and I got the divorce and full custody of my dear son. My ex-husband was ordered to pay $100.00 per month in child support. As long as he paid his support, he could see the baby at certain times. I was terrified of this!

I began to fast and pray that God would never let him see my son. It would never be in my child's best interest. I knew these people would never return him if they ever got their hands on him. I received two checks from him.

On the first Thanksgiving, his sister called to ask if they could have "Junior" for the holiday. Thankfully, Billy had not been consistent in his payments, and I could legally say, "No!"

My dad and I went to the lawyer, asking to have all parental rights taken away. My ex-husband would have to go a solid year without sending payment. The lawyer would put a notice in the newspaper stating his rights were being terminated. If he didn't respond within that year, his rights as a parent would be gone.

Again, God honored my prayers, and in 1975, Billy's rights were legally terminated!

He never tried to get in touch after that. I didn't have to worry anymore! The angels were still with us!

Chapter 9

I worked full-time for three years, walking with God. I was so in tune with Him that I could literally hear Him speak to me. My purpose was to spread His love, hope, and peace and to serve others. He led me everywhere I went.

I was working the 3 p.m.-11 p.m. shift one evening, and it was almost time to clock out. There were thirty minutes left, and the nurse got a call about a patient with cirrhosis of the liver coming to our floor at 10:45 p.m.

It was an inconvenient time to get an admission, but this was an unusual patient. This person had been dying for a month and making an eerie sound that scared everyone. They looked like a skeleton with black skin hanging and had a deep shade of yellow in the eyes. The abdomen was extremely distended and was stretched to its limits.

The patient had been at death's door for a month and was being sent to our floor because the bed was needed for someone else.

I was the aide assigned to get vitals. I had been in the coffee room eating crackers and drinking coffee when the elevator doors opened at the far end of the corridor.

All of a sudden, the loudest crying of a soul I had ever heard got closer and closer. It was an eerie sound, very ghostlike, and it scared the other two aides standing with me. According to the report, this cry had not ceased for over a month.

My friends shivered and said to me, "Thank God this one belongs to you."

As the voice grew closer, an eeriness was felt in the air. I immediately recognized this person's spirit crying out!

The night before, I had been reading the book of Psalms. I read a scripture that stuck with me as I slept. All through the next day, I couldn't stop thinking about it.

Psalms 30:5 says, "For his anger endureth but a moment: in his favor is life. Weeping may endure for a night, but Joy comes in the morning."

The scripture was rolling through my head, and I didn't know why.

I helped get the new patient into bed. When we were alone, I took the patient by the hand, made eye contact, and purposely and warmly introduced myself. The ghostlike cry immediately stopped as the patient looked at me with attentive lucidity.

I asked, "Why are you crying?"

Almost immediately, the reply was, "I'm scared and don't want to die alone. I lived a bad life, and God won't accept me."

"You aren't alone," I said.

As we held hands and tears fell, the patient began to thank me for taking the time to hear and see and validate with dignity. I said God loved them, that their weeping had been heard, and the morning would bring joy.

I said a prayer as we held hands and witnessed a peaceful transition with the most beautiful smile; and noticed serenity and peace had replaced fear and crying.

There was no more fear, only acceptance.

"You're the one I have been waiting on; I'm ready now," the patient said.

I learned the next day that the patient died quietly and in peace just after midnight.

I cried, realizing I had been in the right place where God wanted me and had helped someone find Joy in the morning. All it took was stopping to see a soul in trouble, reacting in love and respect, and giving a dignified end.

I can understand the fear the other nurses and staff felt listening to the eerie ghost-sounding cry. It was unrelenting and very scary. But the human just needed someone to stop and acknowledge their existence and to know they still mattered!

It was a valuable lesson for me. After that, I tried to walk slower through life so that I didn't miss a person who needed help. I consciously chose from that day forward to make eye contact with everyone I passed. Our eyes speak volumes, and sometimes, just making eye contact with a smile lets someone know they have been seen. It can make them feel like they matter.

There were many beautiful encounters in my walk with God as an aide. I spent all my time praying with the dying and giving hope to those who had none. I loved my patients and loved sharing God with them.

Giving to others made all I had been through seem less traumatic. It was also a good way to not dwell on the past but look forward to new chapters with hope and peace in my heart.

Chapter 10

My mother and sister were great with my son and took good care of him when I couldn't. My father and brother were great role models for him, and my son loved all his family very much.

I knew I couldn't support my son on a nurse's aide salary, so I started praying about becoming a nurse. If I went to St. Anthony School of Nursing, it would take me three full years to complete. On the other hand, if I became an LPN, it would take one full year to complete my studies.

My mother and sister seemed to be getting extra attached to my son, and I worried they would try to replace me. I was beginning to feel insecure when I left him with them. For that reason, I chose to go to LPN school because it was the shortest amount of time I would have to be away from my child.

I knew I could make more money as an RN, but there was a restlessness brewing in our home concerning my position as my son's mother.

My mother felt I went to church too much and didn't like it when I always took my son. She also began to cut his hair without consulting me. She was starting to treat him more like her own son and not mine.

Mama also reminded me too often that I needed to date. She'd say it wasn't normal for a girl my age to be so close to God. She even asked me if I was gay once. I was not gay, just not interested in dating. My heart still hurt from all the trauma I had been through.

All her comments began to bother me, and I could sense another war starting.

One night after I got home from work, I wrote God a letter. I said,

Dear God,

Remember when I said I would be married to Jesus until further notice?

Well, I think it's time we talk about my future. My son and I can't live with my parents forever. I want him to have a father of his own. I think it's time I look for a husband. This is what I'd like to have.

I'd like an Italian man with olive skin.

I'd like someone from New York.

I'd like someone who works in health care.

I'd like him to have an unusual last name.

I need him to adopt my son and treat him as his own always.

Thank you, Lord.

I Love You,

Debbie, your daughter

I put this letter in an envelope and addressed it to God in Heaven. It stayed tucked away in my Bible.

After I graduated from LPN school in 1978, I worked at a different hospital's burn center.

The year it took me to become an LPN gave my parents more time with my son, and they were parenting more than me. Mama would tell me I was too young to be a mother. I had missed out on my life, and I needed to live. I should get an apartment, live on my own, and date. I should give power of attorney over to them. She assured me she and my dad would take very good care of my son, that they were stable and made enough money to give him a better life than I could.

While I deeply appreciated how much they embraced and loved him, I could feel myself losing my son to them.

I could see that Mama was more in the parent role, and we began to fight over my child. I told her I wasn't giving him to them. He was my child, and I loved him very much. As soon as I could afford to, I would be taking him to a new life with me.

When I would get him ready for church, she would grab him from me and say he wasn't going. It had escalated to the point three different times where she and my father had me in the bathroom saying, 'You're not taking him to church!"

Again, I was trapped, holding a four-year-old in my arms—this time fighting my parents for him. God was still with me, though, and I knew our time here needed to come to an end soon. I wasn't going to live without my child. And thank God I chose the LPN pathway. I would have lost my son to them had I gone full-time for three years to RN school.

My new job at the burn center had me working all three shifts. I loved what I was learning and was like a sponge, reading and studying everything I could in my new career. I said yes to every opportunity to earn enough money to live.

We were in an unusual situation in the late 1970s as the doctors taught the nurses. We learned to do things under them that other nurses could not do. We definitely did things out of the scope of our practice. They taught us how to cut and excise dead tissue, how to perform escharotomies, and minor surgical skills. They would teach us at the bedside.

I remember assessing a patient who had burns on 90% of his body, all third-degree. His doctor was there and told me to do an escharotomy on his arms.

An escharotomy is done when there is complete constriction of the limb due to swelling of the tissue. An incision must be made through the dead layers to keep the limb from losing circulation and dying, and you must cut until you get to fresh viable tissue with blood.

I said, "I'm a nurse. I can't do that."

He replied, "If I teach you, you can. Now, pick up the scalpel, nurse."

I did as he directed and picked up the scalpel.

"Cut the tissue," he ordered.

I was scared but began to cut the tissue. I went deeper and deeper until I relieved the pressure, and the circulation was restored.

This doctor had served in World War II and loved to tell his war stories to anyone who would take the time to listen. It seemed we were always full of patients and never had enough time to eat or pee, much less listen to his stories. Once he would get started talking, you would just have to be rude and walk away. I felt sorry for him; he appeared to be a very lonely old man.

But he loved to teach and I loved learning.

Chapter 11

My head nurse came to me one day and told me I would attend the annual burn conference, and my airplane ticket had been taken care of. I was shy and embarrassed, but I expressed my gratitude to her. The medical director always told everyone he had handpicked me, and I was his best burn nurse.

It was a good feeling that someone recognized that I had value.

I attended my first burn conference in Denver, Colorado, in 1979. I spent two days attending as many classes as I could, and I learned a lot about the current treatment of burn patients at that time. I learned that the phrase "high blood glucose" meant "impending sepsis" in a burn patient. Sepsis is when a local infection gets into the bloodstream and can be fatal.

I worked the night shift and gave the report to the medical director and those who followed him that day: the oncoming nurses, interns, residents, my head nurse, and the dietician. It was a big crowd.

I told them the patient had a high blood sugar reading, and the medical director asked me what that signaled. I immediately knew the answer but froze! I was scared to speak to him. I turned a deep red and sat silently as the team watched uncomfortably. The medical director was angry that I didn't respond, as he told the team the answer.

I froze because I realized I was scared of him as a man and an authority figure. I saw Billy's father asking me in front of everyone, "Young lady, do you love my boy?"

It brought back emotions I didn't realize I had, and I got so mad at myself that I didn't have the courage to speak up at the moment. Somehow, the lid to my soul jar had been released, and one of the feelings in that jar that had safely resided all these years showed itself. It was called fear and intimidation.

As quickly as I could, I found the doctor in the lounge and told him I was sorry I didn't speak up, and I knew the answer.

He looked me in the eye and said, "I know you did." It took great courage to face him.

As I walked away, I made a conscious decision to speak up and be brave, hold my head high, look people straight in the eye, and not be intimidated by anyone ever again! That morning, my confidence grew. I took the power back that I had given away six years prior! I had given it to people who didn't value me as a human being. They no longer deserved space in my heart or head! It was a powerful moment for me!

Although I had a long way to go, I was beginning to see that I had worth and was learning what self-love and belief in myself looked like. A week or so later, one of our intimidating doctors passed me in the hallway, and I practiced my newfound power.

He rudely yelled, "Nurse, come back here!" I felt belittled by his voice and demeanor.

I bravely turned to face him, looked him deep in the eyes, and said, "Are you talking to me, Doctor?"

Before he could answer, I said, "My name is not 'Nurse!'"

I introduced myself to him, even though he already knew my name. I told him from now on, I expected to be spoken to with the same respect he required of me.

He politely replied, "I'm sorry I offended you."

Everything changed in me that day. I had found a small part of my voice—the voice that had been ridiculed, stifled, shamed, abused, cursed at, tied down, and almost shut out in my late teens—the voice that was buried deep in the soul jar. The voice that had been called a troublemaker. The voice that had been pushed under the rug. The voice that began to realize that it mattered!

Chapter 12

We admitted a patient who had deep, third-degree burns from being engulfed in a fire. This was a very demanding person, and for a few weeks, treated everyone with great disrespect.

I entered the room one night, and the patient began to cry. I asked, "Why the tears?"

"I saw Jesus last night, and he told me to apologize to everyone for being so mean. I'm sorry, Debbie. Forgive my disrespectful attitude, and I love you. Thank you for being so kind to me."

We clasped hands, and I said, "It's okay. It's hard to go through such a traumatic event as you have with such horrendous pain. You have been expressing normal emotions of anger at the loss of your body image and the loss of your independence. At least you are expressing your feelings and not keeping them all inside. I don't take it personally, and I love you, too."

About that time, the cleaning person came in to empty the trash. This patient didn't stop until every single person received an apology. Something was about to change.

It was only a few days later that the patient became septic and was rushed into our intensive care unit. An emergency surgery was performed to cut away as much dead tissue as possible. The legs were the cause and were filled with infection. I was shocked when they came back to our unit that evening. It had spread so quickly and deeply that there was nothing more to be done except bilateral amputation all the way up to the hips.

Because the doctor had to disarticulate both legs all the way up to the hip joints, the buttocks were gone. They came back weighing forty pounds less. I had never envisioned such a sight! They were now half a body and very sick.

The family kept vigil at the bedside as much as we could allow. Unfortunately, the injuries were fatal.

On the evening this patient died, I was present as the family spoke words of love and gave permission to leave. It was hard to let the loved one go, but the family member realized how very tired and sick this patient was, and once given permission to leave, almost immediately, the heart rate dropped, and the patient straight lined on the monitor.

It was a tearful but beautiful moment as quiet sobs were heard. The patient needed that permission to let go. I stood in quiet reverence as soft and heartfelt cries were expressed. It felt like a holy moment.

This person made amends and followed their heart's lead to do the right thing. I thought about how brave and courageous they had been to amend their wrongs and spread love before they died. It is a beautiful memory I carry, and I look forward to finding them on the other side someday with a big hug.

Where does that courage come from in life?

Just as I was only seventeen, when I was running for my life, hearing the gunfire and protecting my son, courage carried me.

As we tap deep into our soul, which I believe is where God abides, we can find anything we need to survive, thrive, and go through our lives!

Courage lives there!

Chapter 13

As I pointed out earlier, my mother was relentless about me getting an apartment of my own and giving her power of attorney. My mother had a good point: if something happened to my son and I wasn't around, she could get him help more easily. And for that reason, I gave her and my father power of attorney for medical.

As a new nurse, I had to prove my worth and work when they asked, so I worked all shifts and never said no. I also got an apartment to live in alone. I had a bed, dresser, and table for the kitchen. I only made less than two dollars an hour, and my rent was close to two hundred a month.

I didn't do well financially on my own. I didn't make enough money to pay the rent, eat, buy gas, or buy clothes for my son. I was in the apartment for four months before I got an eviction notice for not paying my rent.

After being evicted, I slept in my car for a few weeks. I would sneak into my parents' house after they'd left for work and take a shower. I still worked as much as they asked me to, which was a lot of double shifts. At this point, I was thankful my son was safe with my parents.

Another nurse needed a roommate. We started sharing an apartment, so I was able to pay my rent then. But there still wasn't enough money to eat, so I would take uneaten food from the patient trays as often as possible. We also kept sandwiches in the refrigerator for patients. They needed lots of calories to heal, so there was always something I could eat.

I went to work on the 3 p.m.-11 p.m. shift one afternoon, and we had just admitted a patient with another sad story.

Two people were adjusting a television antenna on top of a house on a stormy day. Lightning struck and decapitated one of them, while the other one received life-threatening injuries to the body. Barely alive, we did everything to resuscitate and save the patient.

I was working in the intensive care unit that evening and remember walking in to assess this very critically ill patient who was aware and talking. A family member was there and asked me if he could bring a child in to visit. It was against policy to let minors visit, but my heart made an exception to this one. I felt this child needed to see this person and say what he needed to say.

I wasn't worried about policies at the moment. This child needed to say goodbye to this person, even though they didn't realize it was goodbye at the moment.

I remember watching them both with tears, saying goodbye that night, and hearing the exchange of love between them.

It was the last time they saw each other; he died hours later.

In instances like this, my thoughts always went to my own child. I always went home more thankful than when I had left. Life could change horrifically in just a moment. I always tried to give the same love and grace in life I would want from someone else when it was in my power to do so.

It was always a very busy time in the unit.

In the 1980s, we had the capacity for three intensive care patients, twenty acute care patients, and seventeen rehab patients. We changed each patient's dressing three times a day. We would scrub the wounds with medicated sponges, cut away the dead skin, and redress them with new medicine cream and gauze. It was excruciating for them; they were always medicated with narcotics, but they still felt the pain.

The evening shift changed dressings and applied hand and arm splints to prevent contractures. A contracture is when the skin grows stiff and unmovable, resulting in a frozen and webbed joint. The hand splints would keep their arms in a position for eight hours that would prevent frozen joints. The arm splints pulled the arm away from the body to avoid webbing of the armpit. The splints were also a painful experience but necessary—giving them as much function as possible when the skin grew back.

I took great pride in my job and spent a lot of time educating each patient. It was important to teach them to be independent in their healing process. They fed themselves and held their own water for a drink to take their medication, keeping their fingers and moveable joints moving, preventing contractures. We also padded their eating utensils so they could hold them better with bulky dressings and feed themselves.

In other areas of nursing, you instinctively hold the cup for the patient out of compassion because of the wounds on their hands. It was not helpful to do this here. Many patients would call me cruel for not helping them, and that's when the crucial educational piece would come in.

The more they used those joints, the more natural movement they would have after they left the hospital. If they didn't use them and we did everything for them, they would leave with claws and not be able to bend at the elbow or raise their arms.

Many times, I was called sadistic and cruel. I would pull pictures out and show them what they could leave looking like. Eventually, most patients were on board and complied. If they chose to follow our instructions, they were able to move normally when they left. There were always some who refused.

Being a burn nurse back then wasn't easy. We were always causing pain, and it seemed we were always saying sorry to our patients. It became a word that came out without thinking. It seemed heartless, but the result of leaving that unit and going into a cruel world with as much autonomy as possible would make their life much easier to bear and our goal.

That made burn nursing different.

Chapter 14

One morning, I was taking care of a person who had third-degree burns over 95% of the body. This patient was critically ill and had a deep cavern in the abdomen that we had to clean out. We had to put gloves on that went up to our shoulders. It was a nightmarish sight and horrible to see. I can't adequately describe how gruesome the situation had been; all the while, this person was still alive and aware. Body parts were falling off in my hands as I cleaned the patient's wounds.

It is an indescribable feeling when you are gently cleaning a severely burned hand, and a finger falls off! I remember the first time it happened. I stopped and stared for a minute in shock. I said a quiet prayer and had to keep going.

This patient could open their eyes and shake their head to yes-and-no questions. The mind was still there, which made it more horrifying.

I'd be gently cleaning and apologizing when I looked up to see piercing blue eyes looking at me. It's a sight I can't describe well enough to make anyone understand. Years later, it would torment me in my dreams.

The psychiatrist came in while I was changing their dressings and saw me cleaning the deep cavern. He looked like he would pass out as he asked me how long I'd been doing this. I told him fifteen years at the time.

He said, "How do you do it? How do you handle it?"

Without thinking, I remember telling him, "I just disassociate myself. It's hard, though."

He said, "I understand," and he had to leave the room.

The patient eventually died.

As a teenager, I learned to emotionally remove myself when I was being abused by people who hated me. All I could do was give those feelings away. I gave them to God at the time. With no prior skills to navigate traumatic waters alone, I created the "soul jar," which resided in the depths of my heart.

With the jar in my corner, I found I could stuff as many horrible feelings and experiences as life sent my way deep into the crevices of that jar, which became bigger with time. With the work I was doing, things as indescribable and traumatic could not be explained away. These experiences were too graphic and inhumane and needed to be done, which was part of my job. But it was never easy.

I remember working an evening shift with one of my best friends. We had gotten several people in from a bad accident. Three were under twenty-five years old; they were critical and dying. We had done all we could for them. Within a matter of three hours, we coded all three of them unsuccessfully.

We got their bodies ready for the medical examiner and finished our charting. I looked at my friend with tears in my eyes and said, "I feel like I just need to scream!"

She said, "Me, too!"

"Let's go exploring and find somewhere no one can hear us and do it!"

I found a small closet deep in a therapist's office near our tank room. We each got a pillow and took turns screaming, crying, and laughing into it until we peed our pants! We had found a new way to release feelings effectively. It was an empowering tool if we released them while they were fresh. We didn't have to place them in the soul jar that way. After that, we used the closet many times.

I told the psychiatrist about the scream closet we had created, and he told me to keep using it. It was a healthy way to release these horrifying experiences.

Everywhere I went, I walked with compassion and felt the fears, tears, and pain, but I could not allow myself to feel too deeply. How could I do it otherwise? Maybe I wasn't coping as well as I thought I was. It would catch up with me later on in my life.

It was easy to predict the outcome of most big burns regarding survival. You add the percentage of body-surface burns with their age and pre-existing conditions like diabetes, heart disease, high blood pressure, or obesity. Each condition added a higher chance of death.

For instance, if a forty-year-old man had a third-degree burn of over 70% of his body surface, he had a minus 10% chance of surviving.

When you add pre-existing diseases, the risk increases—if the neck and face are involved, they would likely need the ventilator, which is life support. They were highly likely to die from their burns. It was an accurate formula at the time.

I saw a lot of people who weren't told beforehand they were going to die. I hated seeing that, and it soon became a new mission. I would never let anyone in my care die without being told they were dying and given the opportunity to get their affairs in order. I asked permission from the doctors to tell these patients they were dying. No one was comfortable doing this at the time, but I was. It was just a different kind of continuation of what I had been doing as an aide before I became a nurse.

On one hectic day, our unit was at total capacity with patients. It was my day off, and they called me in to take care of a new intensive-care burn patient. This person had third-degree burns on 100% of the body; the survival rate was zero. They had been burned so deeply that the charred skin crumbled in my hands.

They were on life support with a tube down the throat that was connected to the ventilator; due to burns and swelling in the neck and face. The eyes were swollen shut as the skin stretched to its limits. Lips were swollen so much they turned inside out. They were so swollen from the fluid shift that happened in the body that they weren't even recognizable as a human.

Still alert, they could communicate by shaking their head appropriately to answer yes and no questions.

The thing was, back then, our patients didn't realize how badly they were burned and felt no pain in a situation like this. The nerve endings had all been destroyed, which is why there was no pain with a third-degree burn. The mind was not burned, so most patients maintained the ability to communicate, and unless told, they had no idea how badly they were injured.

After my assessment, I prepared all the gear for a full-body dressing change. I wanted to have a conversation, so I created a padded marker and put paper on a clipboard for the person to attempt to write. The arms and hands were also very swollen. Bulky dressings on her hands made it hard to hold the pen perfectly.

I asked the patient if they realized how very sick they were, and they responded by shaking their head no.

I compassionately told the person that there was not a spot on their body that wasn't burned. I said they had inhaled smoke, and their lungs were severely damaged. The tube in their nose was connected to the ventilator, which kept them breathing and alive.

I added, "All the burns were third-degree, and they would likely die from these injuries."

"When?" the patient wrote.

I told them that twelve hours had already passed and they didn't have long. Pure shock was the response!

"I need a lawyer," the patient scribbled.

I realized they needed more help than I could give at this point. I went to the desk, called the house supervisor, and told her the patient wanted to make a last will and testament. The supervisor brought a lawyer in within an hour. I was a witness.

I then called the chaplain, who prayed with this person. They quietly sat in shock that this was actually happening while I continued my nursing care duties.

After everyone left, the patient motioned to me and wrote, "Thank you for telling me," and died four hours later.

I often thought if I had not followed my heart and carried out my mission, this person would not have known death was there and would have died without getting the affairs in order. I was part of the plan for them to learn their fate.

What a lesson!

I became more determined than ever to ensure everyone knew their survival rate within the first few hours. I could have just been too busy with all the tasks I had to complete within my eight hours with them. Was it really my business anyway? Yes, it was always the answer I came back to.

Someone had to tell these patients. Why not me? Everyone deserved to die with dignity and had the right to know death was at the door.

This one did die with dignity and choice that night. I am proud that I took the time to help in this way. The truth was they were dying, and the clock was ticking whether they knew or not. They almost ran out of time!

Chapter 15

Remember the letter I wrote about God concerning a husband?

I was working the day shift and was assigned to the intensive care unit. One day, I listened to my patient's lungs, heart, and stomach as I performed my assessment. I listened intently, trying to learn what rales and crackles sounded like. The previous nurse had told me this patient was experiencing them.

A male's voice broke my concentration. He said, "You cut your bangs!"

Surprised and embarrassed, I looked up and said, "Yes, I did."

"I like them," he said in response as he winked at me.

I just about melted to the floor. It had been five years since my divorce, and aside from writing the letter to God, I had spent all my time studying, learning, praying, and working. I had been lost in my world and happy with it. I hadn't dated anyone.

Something stirred in me that I didn't ever remember feeling before. This man had entered the room to pick up a patient to take into the tank room for a bath and dressing change. I had been so focused on learning about burn care that I hadn't noticed this guy who had just made my face turn crimson red by winking at me.

As he rolled the patient out the door, I stared until I couldn't see him anymore. The voice I knew so well in my gut told me he would become my second husband! It wasn't too long before he asked me out on a date.

We began to date and fell in love quickly. We had good chemistry and nursing in common. The day he asked me to marry him, I remembered the letter I had written to God.

- I was marrying an Italian man with olive-colored skin.
- He was from New York.
- He was a Registered Nurse.
- He had an unusual Italian last name.

He also told me he wanted to adopt my son the same day.

Everything I asked for, I got! It was another great lesson about what we put out and into the universe to God, whether it be requests or thoughts. I was still very young and looks and chemistry mattered to me. God gave me what I put out there. Those are the only things I asked for; had I asked for more, I do not doubt I would have gotten it.

I was sincerely ready to get my son back and live in the same house as a family. My parents had him for almost a year and didn't want to give him back. They didn't like my choice of a husband because he had shoulder-length hair and wore John Lennon-type glasses. He looked like a damn hippie, my father said. They fought and threatened to take me to court, but I wasn't shrinking away.

The day I picked up my son and his toys, my dad stuck his big finger in my face and said, "Young lady, you better take good care of that boy. If I ever see him with a runny nose, and it looks like you're not caring for him properly, I'll take you to court, and you'll never see him again."

It hurt me deeply that my dad said all those things to me. Just because I was young didn't make me unfit.

Why did he have to threaten me like that? I thought those days were over. From the day I knew I was pregnant, I had done everything in my power to become the best version of myself at every stage, using what I had in my toolbag.

My love for my child was deep, and now all I wanted was a chance to be a family and a full-time mommy to him. I was thankful for my new family. I was so happy to be with him and be his mommy.

My parents loved my son so much, but they weren't grandparents anymore; they were parents. I never wanted it that way, but I appreciated their love for him.

My dad was mad at me for the next six months and would not take my calls or see me. I could see my dad had become my son's father, and it was hard for him to let him go. It was even more challenging to let him go to a "damn hippie."

I will forever appreciate his love for my son. That love gave him a stable foundation in his early formative years that made a difference in his life. My son knew he was loved.

Being in a happy relationship with a man who loved me and my son felt good. We started with humble beginnings in an 800-square-foot house and very little furniture. We had beds, a couch, and a table to eat at. My son had his toys, and we had all we needed then.

It felt good to be secure and just relax in the arms of someone who would protect and love us for the rest of our lives.

Chapter 16

I had left the trauma of my first husband and sat with God for five years. During those five years, I started working at the most traumatic and stressful unit I could have chosen.

I was causing pain to people to heal them. Their cries were always piercing my dreams. The sights I saw would later cause PTSD in my life.

I needed time to slow down and regroup from all the trauma. I had fought off violent people alone. I faced obscene words thrown at me daily. I faced people who thought I was a whore. I fought off people who wanted me dead all because I carried a baby they wanted.

And now, my parents are threatening me. They judged me because I prayed too much. They judged me for going to church too much. They judged me for being too young to be a good mother. They judged me for working too much. They judged me for getting an apartment even though it was my mother's idea. They judged me for not dating, and then they judged me for who I dated. They judged my choice of friends and husband. They even judged me for becoming an LPN instead of an RN.

There was never a time when anyone verbalized being proud of my courage, strength, vision, compassionate heart, ability to defend myself, and unwavering love for my son.

I had a lot to prove to everyone. I needed to prove that I wasn't a slut. I needed to prove that I was a good mother. I needed to prove I was a good human because I didn't think my parents believed me. I needed to prove that I could have a happy home. I needed to prove that I was a good nurse.

My whole purpose became proving I could.

I had been told I couldn't do so much; I subconsciously believed it. I had also been programmed since my early childhood that I could not make wise decisions of the heart.

Everyone tried so hard to quiet the voice deep in my soul that accepted people as they were. The voice that helped me make the choices of the heart, the voice that would lead me, the voice that showed me what I was passionate about, the voice that gave me an option to choose.

As time passed, I wrote my parents a letter and thanked them for all they had given my son and me. They had taken on another child, which wasn't in their plans. They loved and adored my son, and I would be forever grateful to them.

I told them it hurt me that they thought I was unfit to be a good mother. I told them it was very disrespectful when my dad put his finger in my face and threatened to take my son from me if he saw him with a runny nose.

I was simply trying to bridge this separation of time and feelings. I had hoped to be able to talk with them, but that was the beginning of a lifetime of ignoring emotional issues and addressing affairs of the heart with them—they were not equipped to do that.

My mother wrote back that my dad would never apologize, and I just needed to sweep this under the rug. Forget about it. He'll get over it that way. "Don't expect an apology from him," she said.

My dad forgave me, eventually, but for what? For taking back what was mine and never his? I never asked myself that question back then; I just accepted that I was always the one they blamed when things went wrong, and there would be no further discussions on the matter.

With time, my dad learned to respect and love my new husband for how he cared for my son and me. He realized he was wrong to judge my husband by his looks. He eventually got a haircut, which probably helped.

I had missed two periods and was terrified at the thought of bringing another child into this world for someone to threaten me over. I didn't feel equipped emotionally. Between my job and all the feelings making their way out of my soul, I was emotionally drained and had no strength to face any more judgments. It was all still so fresh. I didn't feel like I could control the situation and was scared to death. My parents already thought I wasn't a fit mother, and now if they knew I had another child in my belly before marriage, they would know I was a slut!

How had that feeling escaped from the jar?

The trauma of all I had been through came rushing back at me. I made a choice with my husband to terminate that pregnancy. I got the abortion at nine weeks.

At the time, I couldn't see a way out. I had been told I was a whore, slut, and bitch so much. It hurt to be considered in that light when it wasn't true, or was it?

I knew I was committing murder, and I went into the clinic, begging God to forgive me for what I was about to do. I couldn't face the abuse and name-calling again. I didn't have the strength to.

Life had been violent and traumatic because of judgments and criticisms of what others thought about me and tried to do to me. I felt crippled at the time.

Yes, I was praying to God a lot, but I had shelved the traumatic feelings I had experienced in my short life. They were in a jar that resided in my deepest soul and had become my belief system. But prayer isn't always enough. I needed human help, too.

I got the abortion at 10 a.m. and went to work a very busy 3 p.m.-11 p.m. shift that afternoon. I worked robotically. I was trying not to feel any guilt and remorse over my decision. I had to bury this incident in the jar, very deep within my soul.

I took my mother's previous advice that day and shoved this under the rug; it would be twenty years before I allowed myself to remember or feel what I had done. I tucked it deeply inside my soul where shame, sadness, and memories of unrelenting pain lived.

After that, I went to work part-time, working three days a week to be home more with my son. Being a good mother to him was the most important goal in my life, and I didn't feel I could be a good mother and work forty hours a week.

Watching my mother go to school and working full time had a profound effect on me because she was always gone. When she was there, she wasn't present. I never felt real love from her, and it was always conditional. I felt loved if I behaved properly, kept my mouth shut, and performed as I was told. It was hard to be silent when I felt betrayed, unseen, lied to, or ridiculed.

She would say things to me in manipulative ways that always made me feel bad. I would react, and then my dad would get mad and slap, spank, or yell at me.

It was hard for me to respect my mother because she didn't seem to respect me. My father always had her back, though; no matter the situation, he would demand I respect her. My mother didn't always tell the truth. I hated it and would speak up about it.

I could easily see through a person and tell when they were lying. I learned to read a person very early on in life. I would watch people everywhere I went and study their body language. It became an interesting hobby that I still do today. I'm always watching and hardly miss anything around me.

I could see right through my mom, and I didn't respect her for not being real or authentic all the time. She was one person in public and a different one at home. I felt she put a fake face on around others. She could turn any situation around, and I always seemed to be the one who got blamed for everything in our family. She was a master at manipulation.

I grew up hating lies and fakery because of this.

Remembering all this was why not being home with my kids was something I could not compromise on. I had been told I was a lousy mother by my ex-husband and his family and my parents, and I needed to be there in their lives so I could raise well-loved children. It's the only way I knew how to do it.

My new husband, Donny, agreed that I should go part-time. I had things to prove, after all. I eventually worked only every other weekend when we decided to add another baby to our family.

We decided to marry in 1980, and later added a daughter. She was so beautiful. I felt euphoric with my new family. I bonded well with her and my son; he was proud and happy to have a new sister. He was a very good brother to her.

We spent lots of time taking walks to parks, swimming all summer, watching my son play soccer and baseball, and all the things I thought healthy families did. We got a dog and a ferret, and my life was working out in a happy way.

Chapter 17

I started volunteering in churches when my daughter was two. I taught Sunday School and became the children's church director in several churches.

I loved the young preschool age and focused on that since my daughter was at that age. I wrote and directed many plays that we would perform for the church. I would get big refrigerator boxes and shape and paint them for props and scenery. It was a fun program for them.

I set up a program where I trained preteen and teens to be teacher's assistants. We met every Saturday for four weeks. They had to attend all four classes to volunteer. This requirement excused them from the church services that bored them. This requirement also helped them grow confidence as they learned to lead others, mentor, and love the little ones.

I was very strict and had policies they had to follow. They could only be in my program if they were prepared each Sunday and followed the rules. They needed an open heart to God and a willingness to grow and accept every child in love and not show favoritism. We grew a program of over a hundred kids each Sunday in all the churches I volunteered at.

I always felt that if we could show children real love and acceptance at an early age, they would have a memory or foundation to return to when life got hard for them, and for the most part, life was already hard. They were like hungry little birds, soaking up the attention, snacks, and love.

It broke my heart to see how many unloved and hungry children were among us. The church was proud to bus the inner-city kids in, yet nobody took care of their needs when they got there.

Before I got deeply involved, I noticed all these bused-in children that the adults would yell at and talk about because they smelled or were so hungry. I saw children ask for more during snack time, and they were scolded and told no.

When I saw the need, I went to the children's pastor and told him what I was seeing and wanted to do. That's when I established the program to train the older kids to teach the younger ones. I would have regular staff meetings with all the helpers. The adults and the teens had to follow policies.

I was in a hallway with the children one Sunday when I witnessed one of my adult helpers grab a little girl by the hair and, with a cruel voice, yell at her as he shoved her back in line. This guy was also a Deacon of the Church, and this was one of the largest metropolitan churches in town in the 1980s.

Without thought, I looked at him and told him to take his hands off that child and get out of my program!

He said, "You can't kick me out!"

"I just did, and don't you ever lay another hand on one of these children again," I said as I stared at him. He left, and I expected to get dismissed by the pastor from the program myself, but I didn't.

I knew I wouldn't be anywhere forever, and my goal was always to train a replacement who would carry the heart of God and keep the training going if I couldn't. I started noticing many things happening in the church that I couldn't support. I left and went to start another program, training my replacement each time.

I would hold a summer Vacation Bible School in the deep inner city, known for heavy gang activity. I did this for three years. I brought several of my trained teenagers to help. Food was always as important as love. If we said, "I love you," without feeding them, it meant nothing.

We helped a lot of children, and we never had any trouble from the neighborhood. I was shocked at how many young children carried beepers, and it was such a blessing to see their sweet faces soften when they saw the love we were extending to them.

Love looked different to them—a cup of Kool-Aid and an Oreo cookie said "I love you" in a way they weren't used to. We took time out and enjoyed eating cookies while we stared at the clouds together. It created an atmosphere that fostered laughter and jumping around; the sugar helped, too!

Even if it was only for a week, we were showing God to them, and it felt good to see the hope arise in their hearts and the smiles on their faces. Sometimes, all we have is a day or a week, maybe even a few years, to make a difference.

If we walk slowly enough, that voice will always lead us to those we can help. Sometimes, it's paying for someone's purchase at the store when they are counting their pennies. I purposely go to thrift stores weekly for someone I can help.

I will watch someone add the total in their head and put things back. I often approached them and told them I'd like to buy them whatever they needed, including the items they returned. They always ask why. I always reply because I care and quietly assure them it's okay.

We all need Hope, and we all need to know that we Matter!

Over the years, I went to the Nazarene and Baptist churches, where I started my programs, too. As long as children needed instruction, I was the leader. Going to church was a big part of raising my kids. I enjoyed showing them how to give back to those less fortunate. I always tried to be the same person at home as I was everywhere else. It was important to me that my kids be taught through a good, honest example.

Looking back on my life, I realize that raising my children was my absolute favorite time. They were so much fun to raise and a joy to watch as they matured into wonderful young men and women.

Donny didn't go to church with us. He was raised Catholic but didn't mind that I wasn't raising them in the Catholic church. He knew God answered my prayers and would come to me quite often asking for a car prayer, a money prayer, or a heart prayer of some sort. He worked many double shifts to earn enough money for me to stay home. I would save and put one hundred dollars a week away for Christmas or vacation. We always took a nice two-week trip each summer as a family.

Early on in my marriage, I began to feel an unsettled feeling with my husband. That voice inside me was starting to sound an alarm that not all was as it seemed in our marriage.

Deep in my soul, I didn't feel I could trust him. I was new to relationships and naïve, but I was so in love that I tried to look past many glaring red flags.

We began to fight over certain behaviors he would do that made me feel insecure. Our fights always escalated to me screaming and crying and begging him to stop flirting or doing the things that eventually destroyed the marriage. Donny always turned things around and blamed my screaming on our fights. I would cry and voice my concerns, and he would get mad and say I was making things up. He always blamed me for being jealous, but that feeling never went away.

He started taking scuba diving lessons and had planned a trip to Cozumel. I didn't plan to go, but I was okay with him going until I got a phone call from his scuba dive master one morning. He asked to talk to my husband, who was asleep. I asked if I could take a message. He just wanted to ensure Donny and Lucy still planned on rooming together. I said, "I'm not sure who Lucy is."

"The master told me she is your husband's partner."

I said, "I'll have to check and have him call you."

When Don woke up, I told him his dive master had called and needed to confirm that he and Lucy were still rooming together.

"Yeah, we are."

I asked who she was.

He innocently said, "She was just someone I work with." He blew it off and tried to make me feel crazy for thinking it was a problem.

"You didn't think that would be an issue with me?"

"Why do you always have to make things worse than they are? She is just a good friend." His manipulation made me crazy.

After he had left, I woke up knowing I needed to go to Cozumel to save my marriage. I sent the kids to my parents, got on a plane, and surprised him at the resort.

Of course, I messed everything up with the sleeping arrangements. The dive master was upset with him and had to rearrange everyone to get her out of my husband's room. They had already had one night together. Her panties and bra were hanging in the shower.

I was naïve then, but I was sure I had interrupted something that should not have happened, even though he denied it. He took advantage of my forgiving and naïve heart. I spent many years feeling insecure, wondering if he was being faithful to me. I never caught him other than this time, but that voice that guides me through life always told me that he wasn't behaving.

It wasn't until many years after our divorce that a family member confirmed that she had slept with Donny on a visit to our house. It seemed that some abnormal behavior would always come up, and I knew in my heart that my feelings weren't lying to me.

Chapter 18

My happy home was not so healthy.

Raising my kids in a healthy and happy home was the most important thing in the world to me. They were my purpose, and I was glad to be home with them. I loved being their mother. They were both beautiful souls; I have always been very proud of them.

My son was very outgoing and funny. He was always a leader in school and had many friends. We always laughed a lot with him.

One evening, while I was at work, I received a call from Donny telling me my son had walked home from school that afternoon and been kidnapped.

My son was in the fourth grade. Two men had picked him up by a park near our house. He noticed a car following behind him and started running when the passenger got out and grabbed him. The man held him in his lap in the front seat while another man drove.

My son said he began to pray and asked God to get him out of there. He knew they would kill him if he didn't.

They were stuck in traffic about five miles from our home when my son elbowed the man in the side and kicked him in the scrotum. He then opened the door and ran for his life. He went to the nearest place of business and called his dad, who immediately went to pick him up.

I was terrified as I cried out to God while leaving work and driving home to be with my family. I thanked him for saving my son's life and for bringing him safely back to us. I was shocked and couldn't believe this had happened. It was a terrifying time, but God was still taking care of him.

The night before, I had been reading Jeremiah 29:11, which said, "I know the plans I have for you, says the Lord. Plans to prosper you and not harm you, plans to give you hope and a future."

This verse was a tremendous promise from God about my son's life. It was another miracle! The angels were still with him!

My daughter was a big talker and had many friends growing up. She was a joy to have in my life.

She became a ballerina when she was three and was so cute to watch in her recitals. For eight years, I looked forward to her spring recitals.

She was always a director in life and would help those kids who got out of line. She was always the school teacher when the neighbor kids visited, and they were the students. It was fun to watch her send them in the hall for breaking a rule. Even though it was all play, she played seriously. She was always in charge. She was a gift from God that I will always treasure.

My son graduated from high school in May 1992. It seemed Donny had been waiting for that moment. He came to me one morning in June with some paperwork and told me he was divorcing me. Donny said he didn't love me anymore and was leaving that day. He had prepared a letter stating how much child support and alimony he would give me. He was being generous. He said he would carry me on his insurance for one year, and then I would have to get my own.

We had been married for twelve years. I was shocked! I didn't believe it. How could he do this? It was all so very sudden, with no warning! He literally woke up and said we needed to talk, presented me with his proposal, took a shower, left, and never returned home again.

I cried and begged him to change his mind. I begged him to go for couples counseling, but he said, "No, my mind is made up."

I was absolutely devastated. I didn't want a divorce. I loved him! We were a family! I needed him to change his mind!

Donny had clearly made up his mind before this, and with the help of his new lover, there was no going back for him. He left and went straight to her. He moved next door to the lady he was having an affair with. She was a new nurse who worked with him. They got married eight weeks later before our divorce had a chance to get cold.

Donny denied the affair. He came to me one day and said, "You will probably get a phone call from my friend's husband.

He thinks we've been having an affair, and he wants to talk to you."

I said, "Hmm, imagine that! I'll be delighted to hear what he has to say!" I wish he would have called, but he never did.

Don was still manipulating me with his lies.

I had been stupid throughout the years, ignoring what I felt were signs of infidelity. But this time, I could not ignore them. Donny was in love with her and told me so later.

I spent the next year crying, not eating, trying to figure out what I'd do next, and spending as much time as I could with my daughter before I went back to work full-time. My dad was there again, giving me emotional support. He had grown to love my husband as his own son and was devastated, too. My dad said he tried to reason with my husband, but his heart had already gone elsewhere.

I depended on my dad a lot. He would come over, sit on my porch swing, and listen to me cry. I still hear his great advice, as he told me, "Debra, hold on. You never know what's up around the bend!"

I repeat those words out loud quite often, and they still comfort me. It's true, too. Life has a way of working out!

We all have lessons to learn. I had lessons in this marriage. I grew in ways that may have taken longer in other circumstances. I had expected to be married to this man for the rest of my life. Now, I am thankful he divorced me.

I didn't know what being healthy looked like then. It took all of that and more to teach me.

Chapter 19

I had just showered when my son came home and proudly announced that he had joined the United States Marines. He had been out of high school for a month or so.

I was shocked and didn't expect this! I had always prayed he wouldn't have to ever go to war. My deepest fear was him joining and going to war and never coming home again. I was scared to death as I screamed, cussed, and yelled, "How could you do this to me? I can't lose you, too!"

The Gulf War was going on. My reaction was horrible, and I could see his face fall as I disappointed him by reacting so emotionally. This young man was my son whom I loved and adored, and all I could think of was how he could be mistreated, hurt, and possibly sent home in a body bag!

I was devastated again.

I refused to talk to the Sergeant who had recruited him. He called often, trying to speak to me, but there was no undoing this, and I had to accept it.

My marriage and son were leaving me at the same time.

After I calmed down, my son told me he would be getting on an airplane in November to go to San Diego, California.

His sister and I had three months to celebrate their birthdays, as well as Thanksgiving and Christmas. We would do all the holidays at a different time before he left. We celebrated each time with great intentions, knowing it was our last time together for a while.

I cooked big meals with all his favorite foods on different October weeks to celebrate our holidays. It was a memorable time with good bonding, and I'm so glad we did it.

My son got my daughter a new trampoline for her birthday. She loved it, and they spent much time together on it before he left. It would make me so sad to see them out there talking and jumping because I knew the time we had left with him was short.

My heart broke for my daughter. She adored her brother, and he was good for her. They loved each other very much. We needed him here, but he needed to grow into a man his way, and I had finally accepted that. We made every day count while he was here, and I was thankful I didn't have to work full-time yet.

Five of his friends came to the airport the evening he left to say goodbye. In the 1990s, you could still go to the gate and see them off. I watched him with great pride and deep love as he interacted with his friends. My son was so loved, and it was hard to see him go. I hugged him long and hard one last time before he boarded the plane.

That precious little baby, whom the angels and I had guarded and protected so often, had grown into a beautiful human who felt confident enough to get on an airplane to fulfill one of his dreams. He had written about becoming a Marine in the third grade. He had grown his wings and needed me to let him fly away.

It was hard to let him go, but I had to. I cried all night after he left. I laid him in God's divine arms, where he had resided his whole life. I asked God to give him the strength and power to endure everything thrown at him for the next three months.

When I couldn't sleep, I would give him to God again. I trusted that God would take good care of him like He always had.

My daughter and I wrote to him every day, and he wrote back. It was so good to see his handwriting on the first letter I got from him. I still have his letters. I missed him so much!

His birthday was coming up. He loved iced sugar cookies, and I asked in a letter if I could send him some for his birthday. He wrote back and said, only if you send enough for everyone. He said he would be punished if I didn't send enough. He gave me a number, and I spent a whole day making over 300 cookies, wrapping them, and mailing them to him the next day. They arrived on time, and his drill instructor was happy he had enough to share with the others.

As in school, my son was a leader throughout the Marines. He always had goals and always met them. He got promoted quickly, and God kept him from war.

During his five-year tour, he was stationed in California. He became the General's driver and attended special events in Beverly Hills and Hollywood, where he met some stars.

He had been away for three years. I remember missing him so much and being unable to sleep one night. I turned the television on around midnight. Much to my surprise, my son was on TV dancing on Jenny McCarthy's show, Singled Out! I sat straight up in bed, so very proud and happy.

It was such a happy and beautiful gift! He looked happy and so handsome as he flirtatiously danced past Jenny McCarthy. He was always full of surprises and fun.

In August of that year, my parents came over and announced they were moving to Las Vegas, Nevada. My jaw dropped, and I was devastated as I realized I was losing the last of my support group. They were putting their house up for rent and would leave within the next month.

I cried as I thought about how lonely it would be without them. My daughter and I would be all alone in the city now. I was angry that they would leave me at such a vulnerable time.

While I needed their emotional support, I had some growing to do that required me to find a new way to survive. It was the first time I was actually on my own in life. I was scared to death!

Chapter 20

Like a rolling stone, my daughter and I changed churches again. This time, we chose the Baptist church. I needed to become involved with a singles group and heard they had a good one. I was so embarrassed to admit that I was single. At the time, I had no desire for another relationship. But I needed a new support group, and this looked like an excellent place to start.

Walking into that room for the first time took a lot of courage. I was shaking. I made some good friends who helped me get to the next stage of my life. I just needed to be around people who understood what I was going through. I needed a social group where I felt safe.

After attending for a few months, I noticed there wasn't any kind of program for divorced or widowed people. If I need something like this, others must, too.

One day, I went to the group's pastor and asked why there wasn't a program for divorced people. He said it was because they didn't have a teacher.

"I can teach it," I said. That's when I started a program to help navigate men and women through loss, whether it be divorce or death.

The class was very beneficial and gave me a new support system of like-minded people. It was successful and grew tremendously by word of mouth. I taught the class for two full years.

My goal was to help people move through their pain, feel their feelings, and grow. It was not a place to bash anyone or remain victimized. I taught them that to heal the pain, you must feel it! There was no other way around it. You just had to walk right through it!

Just as I was causing pain to my patients at work, they were healing. As a burn begins to grow new tissue, the nerve endings rejuvenate. When those nerve endings are being cleaned, it hurts like heck. There are a couple of weeks when the pain is so severe they scream out. They beg you to stop—even though they are medicated with painkillers!

If the patient holds on and endures it, the skin magically covers those nerve endings, and the pain eventually disappears. It's the way our body works.

Likewise, if we talk about our pain, cry when we need to, feel it, name it, look deep at what caused it, hold on, and change some behaviors and patterns, we magically feel better one day. Burying it causes problems later on in life. If you feel it while it's identifiable and fresh, it's much easier to let it go.

I knew this well because of my soul jar. Feelings surfacing from my first marriage caused me to react to situations in my second marriage. Insecurities would arise because of fear. Fear was an experience my young adolescent knew all too well and had to stash away in the jar because it was so big and terrifying. Any time it looked like I was losing my second husband, fear would arise, and over time, it had grown more powerful and much uglier.

When my parents thought I was a bad mother and verbalized it, fear surfaced. I was scared to death to lose my son and husband. Had I dealt with the feelings of being shot at, threatened, and abused when they were fresh, I could have released their power.

While the pattern looked familiar, some feelings I was projecting onto my new husband didn't belong there. One way or another, if we don't deal with our problems, they will follow us until we do.

You can wake up one day so angry, sad, and depressed and not be able to tell anyone why. You just want to run away to a cave and never return. You can find yourself screaming and short-tempered at those who did nothing wrong—even though you think you screwed that lid on tight. The stresses of this world are what loosens it. You can't control that. All you can do is try to put a name to the deep feelings you are going through and work on retrieving your power in life.

In teaching the divorce recovery class, I learned that we had all been through rejection, infidelity, abuse, abandonment, and loss. As humans, we share many commonalities. We all cry, feel pain, get hungry, and want to feel safe. Occasionally, we all need someone to hold our hand and tell us it will be alright.

I led these people on the road to recovery with empathy and compassion and led myself to a healthier place as well.

Keep your head up. As my father told me so many times, you just never know what's up around the bend!

Chapter 21

The first Christmas without my husband or son in 1992 was very lonely. I had to work the evening shift, and my daughter stayed with Don and his new wife. She and I celebrated early that morning before I left for work. It was hard to leave her with him, and I didn't want to be at work when she was without me on this once very happy holiday.

We were busy as usual, and I was changing dressings in the tank room. The tank room was large, with several tubs for bathing, and had all the supplies needed to change the dressings.

We had music on, and it was fun to rock out with the patients. It was also very therapeutic for everyone. On days when we had time, my best friend and I would make evening gowns out of Surgifix gauze, put them on over our scrubs, get a 60cc syringe for our pretend microphone, and turn the music up super loud. We would go from room to room, serenading the patients. We called ourselves the Flamettes! She, another nurse, and I would harmonize and sing songs to them. I saw patients laugh who hadn't in months.

I was always looking for ways to lighten the mood and bring some joy to the patients. That evening on Christmas, I had already done about twenty dressing changes. The last patient came in. The music was on as Bing Crosby crooned, "I'm Dreaming of a White Christmas."

This person was saved for last because the wounds dripped more goop and drainage than any other burn I had ever seen. Cupfuls of thick yellow goop would fall to the ground, on you, and everywhere if you didn't have a strategy beforehand.

I had put an extra gown over my scrubs, a plastic apron, a mask, a surgical hat, and gloves, and prepared for the slimy adventure. I really can't do justice in describing this because it wasn't normal. I also had plastic on the floor to make clean-up easier afterward.

I extended my greeting and noticed a sad expression. I asked what was on their mind. After a pause, the response was, "I have been thinking about my life today."

The patient started talking about it being Christmas and said it was the first Christmas they'd spent inside in a long time.

My heart began to break for this unattractive sight of a human. As I worked, I listened and encouraged them to keep talking.

"Yeah, do you know how long it's been since I've had a hug from another human?"

The minute those words were spoken, the voice that guides me through life tugged at my heart, and I knew I would have to hug this person tonight!

"How long has it been?"

"Thirteen years ago, I lost everything and everyone in my life."

My heart fell when they told me their story, and the voice that guided me whispered, "Debbie, this person needs a hug," and I knew I was about to get gooped!

I also knew what loneliness felt like and how not having hugs can cause you to crave them. I also knew what it felt like to be all alone in the world, and I never wanted to withhold something that could make a difference in someone else's life.

My compassion won out, and as I finished the dressing change, I reached out and gave this human a heartfelt hug. "Merry Christmas," I said.

Surprised and overjoyed, an immediate transformation was seen on their face as they skipped out of the tank room so happy!

This person had been seen!

This person had been heard!

For the first time in thirteen years, they were validated and felt as though they mattered, all because of a conversation and hug.

They spent the next hour going up and down the hallway with a huge smile, greeting as many patients and staff as possible, saying, "Merry Christmas!"

My best friend came in as I was cleaning up. She said, "Hey, what's up with Jimmy Stewart out there jumping up and down and telling everyone Merry Christmas?"

"I gave him a hug."

She looked at me and said, "Eww!"

I saw how one kind gesture had changed another person that night. It's not always pretty or comfortable for us to reach out and make a difference. It reminded me again of my purpose, to intentionally love all humans. I was glad I did something no one else was going to do. This person was still someone who got hungry, cried, wanted a bed to sleep in, wanted safety, and needed love.

We all need to know we matter. I knew this as well as anyone. I was learning that I mattered, too, and all the while, I helped make others feel seen. We never know what our fellow humans have gone through. When we prejudge, we limit what we can give and what others can receive.

So many doors are closed through judgment. Everyone matters, every culture matters, every religion matters. Isn't our purpose to spread love, not hate? We are all fellow humans, walking on the same ground and sharing a planet with each other. We are all doing our best to survive and just to be happy.

Slow down, take time, and be aware. People need you. Ask yourself what you can do to change the world where you live—one person at a time!

I was taking care of a person who had been in an accident and was in our intensive care unit for a couple of months. I took care of this patient every evening. Depression had set in, and this one uttered a few words. I had done everything to try to pull them out of their shell.

One evening, a couple of their friends were visiting. I noticed the patient was talking and was so happy they were engaging the visitors. The nurse buzzer went off, and the patient said there were deep boogers in their nose. I detected a spark, a bit of humor in their voice, and decided to have fun with them. I entered the room with my twelve-inch Q-tips to pick boogers!

I had blown a glove up and put it under my arm to slowly release it in the room. I announced I was here to pick boogers! The friends giggled, and I thought, "OK, this will be fun."

I bent over and began to pull out five-inch boogers from the nose. As I pulled one out, I pushed on the blown-up glove, and it sounded like I had farted loudly! The friends, without pause, burst into laughter as they said, "Your nurse just farted!"

My patient began to laugh and didn't stop for fifteen minutes! It was a beautiful moment watching the deep belly laugh happen. They all found great pleasure at my expense that night. The patient found a glimmer of hope that life wasn't over and there might be a future after all.

Sometimes, we need to let our walls down and just "be" with someone. When we take ourselves too seriously, we miss opportunities to lighten a way for someone else.

I learned through all my dark days that laughter made my day so much easier to bear. While some may regard this as inappropriate, I witnessed a human come back from a very dark place through laughter!

Chapter 22

My son had been in boot camp for three months when my daughter and I flew to San Diego, where we proudly watched him become a United States Marine! He had put on weight and was quieter. I could see he had been through a lot. He was happy and content. He had made lifelong friends there and introduced me to some of them. He would be in California for the next several years.

It was time for me to find a full-time job with benefits. The time was rapidly approaching when I had to get health insurance on my own. I went to my head nurse and told her what I needed. She sadly said nothing was available.

I began to search for jobs in Las Vegas, Nevada. I had talked to a recruiter and could interview on a Monday. I had just enough money in the bank to buy a ticket to get to Vegas for the interview. I prayed and told God I needed a sign from Him.

My question was whether I should stay in Oklahoma or go to Vegas, where my parents were. I needed to decide by the end of the week whether to buy the ticket or the price would increase.

It was Friday morning, at 9:00 a.m., and I had just sat down by the phone to make my purchase when it rang. It was my head nurse asking me to come in and talk about a full-time position they were creating just for me. She wanted me to start the first Wound Care Team in Oklahoma. It would be day-shift, full-time with benefits. I could start on Monday! I couldn't believe it! In the nick of time, another miracle just for me dropped out of the sky! It was a dream job and one I had trained for. I would be working under one of our Burn Doctors, who would become the medical director of the wound care team.

I had an excellent rapport with the nurses and doctors all over the hospital, and they quickly learned to trust me as the expert in Wound Care. I had a cart filled with dressing supplies that I pushed around the hospital. When a wound needed help to heal, the Wound Care Team would be consulted. After assessing the patient and wound, I would discuss a treatment plan with the doctor and write out instructions.

I would return every day and carry out the treatment until that wound was healed. We had a very high success rate in healing. In fact, we always healed the wounds we were given.

I started the first week alone, and then they added a burn tech due to the high volume of consults we were getting. It soon became more work than two people could do in eight hours. Word got out fast across the hospital, and we got swamped. Within the first month, we had to add another nurse and two burn techs.

We consulted on every kind of wound imaginable: car accidents, open heart wounds, bed sores, diabetic ulcers, spider bites, cellulitis, leg wounds from open heart surgery, nonhealing amputations, flesh-eating bacteria, and radiation burns, just to name a few.

We stayed busy and had a lot of fun healing the wounds. Having a good crew to work with was fun when everyone knew their stuff. Being a part of such a respected team and considered an expert felt good. We were very good at our job, and it didn't take long before every doctor heard about us and consulted our services. It was another gift I had received, a job I knew a lot about and allowed me to travel all over the hospital and talk to everyone.

I worked at this hospital for two years, running the team.

We eventually merged with another hospital, and they wanted their own Wound Care Team. I also started one for them. That hospital was on the other side of town, so there was a lot of driving. It was nice to get out in the sunshine instead of being stuck inside the hospital all day.

I worked in both hospitals until the new one became busy. Most days, I was alone as the only Wound Care Team member, which got lonely.

I began dating a year after my divorce from Donny. Dating definitely taught me what I didn't want in a man. I met a lot of manipulators and users. Every person I went out with had to pass a test in my head: Could I see them in my family with my kids and future grandchildren? Even though I dated a couple of guys for a bit, nobody passed that test. It was important to bring someone into my life who would effortlessly blend into my children's lives and love them just like I did. Family life was still significant to me and always would be. I still wanted a happy home more than anything. I always wanted a place my children could come back to and feel loved.

Being a mother was still the most important role I had. I desperately wanted to be happily married so my children would have a place to go for Thanksgiving and Christmas. Family life was everything to me. I loved and cherished my children.

Since I had begun to date, I sat with God again one evening and began to tell him what each man I had met had shown me. I had found so many deal-breakers, but I wanted to be happily married. It was a goal in my life. I didn't enjoy being alone, and I wanted a partner to grow old with and share the ups and downs of life.

I told God I'd like a European man next. I decided to look outside of healthcare this time. My reason for this was that the cheating of my second husband did indeed affect my heart.

I wanted to go somewhere I hadn't gone yet. I asked for a businessman. Of course, I needed him to be easy on the eyes. I needed him to have stability and to want to protect and take care of me. I had been walking alone for so long in my life that I craved someone to protect and adore me. I wanted a family man who would embrace my children as his own and love our future grandchildren.

I joined a West Coast swing dance club and began taking lessons. It was a lot of fun, and there were a lot of businessmen there. Sometimes, you have to change your scenery to get what you want, which can help God answer your prayers quicker. Until now, my scenery has existed in hospitals, which wasn't bad. I just wanted to experiment and maybe break a few rules.

My confidence had grown. I was learning to trust myself more to know what I needed. I had begun the long journey of realizing—and then trying to believe—that I mattered. I was surprised at how little I believed this. I had been silenced my whole life and punished for feeling my feelings.

I remember driving to work one morning before I had my new wound care job. I was sad about leaving my daughter, who wasn't feeling well. I was sad, angry, felt defeated, and depressed. I didn't want to be taking care of others when my own kid needed me. I was crying as I drove to work and telling God how mad I was and that I couldn't do this anymore! I was tired of the loneliness and frustration of being a single mother. I didn't want to face the world that day. I needed a hug from a human.

Suddenly, I realized I was having a pity party, and no one deserved the dark energy I would be bringing to my job, especially me.

One of my favorite books I loved teaching children, and my own, was "The Little Engine That Could." I began to say, "I think I can, I think I can, I think I can," over and over as I cried off all my makeup. I was a mess. It wasn't long until I changed the words to, "I know I can, I know I can, I know I can. I can do this!"

I felt a shift in my feelings, and a smile came to my face as I regained more of my power and pulled into the parking garage. I cleaned my face as best I could and walked into work, glowing from a deep cry. My eyes were a little puffy–I just called it allergies–but it felt like a ton had been lifted from my heart.

I was assigned to give medications that day. The med room was right by the nurse's desk, so I saw everyone who came in. That day, every doctor who worked in our unit, which was seven doctors at the time, came in. Each doctor hugged me and welcomed me back to work without thinking about it. They each told me how great it was to see me!

Only God knew how much I needed to not only feel love but also get so many hugs in one day! He was still taking care of me as I took the steps I needed to assist Him in my growth.

I needed to remain courageous and put myself out there. It would have been easy for me to call in that morning because my daughter was sick, but I needed the courage to go to the place where He could bring the humans to me for the hugs I needed.

Our thoughts have power! We can create success or failure with them. Our beliefs are powerful. "I think I can. I think I can. I think I can!" I still had a lot to prove.

The greatest person who needed convincing the most was me! It would be a lifelong journey of learning that I could and that I really mattered.

In the year of 1995, I received a morale boost when I won Nurse of the Year in the Burn Center, Wound Care, and Hyperbaric Center. It was a great gift, and they made a big banner across the front of the unit's entry with my name on it. It was a great honor, and I was very proud to accept and be chosen for this.

My parents were visiting me, and I brought them to the unit to show them the remodeling they had recently done to our unit. As we walked in, my dad saw the sign first and smiled so big. It was fun to show them I was good at something and see their reaction.

Chapter 23

As I said earlier, I started the Wound Care Team at the new hospital and worked alone most days. Our first office was in the surgical unit in a room with no windows in the basement.

When I was through with the dressing changes throughout the hospital, I would sit in the office waiting for consults to come in. That got old and depressing. Although I had made acquaintances and was friendly with everyone, I had no one to talk to or laugh with to relieve stress or eat lunch with. I could feel myself getting depressed because of this.

I started helping the enterostomal therapy nurse and covered this care at the new place as well. That gave me more patients, but this hospital didn't present the challenging wounds the other one did, and I was getting a bit bored and lonely. I needed a working partner. They didn't justify it because the load wasn't as great. I spent two whole years at this place, and I loved my job, and I loved a challenge.

Every other weekend, I had to carry three pagers—one for each hospital for wound care and one for enterostomal therapy. If there was an admission for any of these services, I was paged and called in to take care of the problem.

In the meantime, I was learning to dance at the dance club. I still met lots of people and enjoyed it. Since I wasn't a drinker, it was a fun and safe way to have an active social life that didn't require me to hang out in nightclubs. There were men there, but no one who made me do a double-take until one day in early August 1997.

I had just danced with someone and saw a friend who had been battling cancer sitting down. I went to talk to her. As I walked toward her, I noticed a very handsome man with the most beautiful green eyes looking at me as he stood by her. We made eye contact, and I remember thinking, "Who is that?" Wow! He was definitely a head-turner! She introduced us, and I knew I wanted to find out more about who he was. I asked him to dance.

We danced and sat down together. He was quiet, and I did the pursuing. He was divorced, had been in the Air Force for thirty years, and had recently retired. He was working as an international recruiter, placing people in government contracts.

I watched him as he walked away and back again, walking like he was in charge of the whole room. He exuded confidence and was the most handsome man I had ever seen! He also carried a strong blend of Polish and German heritage, which was very European and was precisely what I had asked for.

I invited him for a root beer float, and he accepted. There was a Coit's drive-in down the road, and they had the best root beer floats. Little did I know how much he loved them. We sat for hours talking. He told me about many of his Air Force stories, travels, and family. I felt like I had known him forever and didn't want the night to end.

After our next date, I accidentally left a key in his truck that I needed the next day. It had fallen out of my purse when I stuffed it under his seat the night before. I looked his name up in the phone book and called him since we hadn't exchanged numbers yet. I had to pick the key up, and as I drove into his neighborhood, that voice that tells me what's next in life said this will be your new neighborhood. You are going to marry this man!

We began to date and fell in love quickly. When you know, you know, and I'd already been told!

He traveled a lot all over the nation. I took a few trips with him, and we enjoyed each other tremendously.

He had three grown children: a son and two daughters. He also had a beautiful, adorable, and very smart little granddaughter with whom I fell in love the moment I greeted her! She was two years old and had the sweetest voice. She sang a lot, and I was just enamored by her! She was beautiful with her black hair and brown eyes! She stole my heart the moment we met, making me love him even more!

We would try to blend five children, a gorgeous granddaughter, and later another grandson. We decided to get married in Eureka Springs, Arkansas, in March of 1998. I was very content and so happy to become his wife, forever this time, and live a life of adventure.

I also became a Catholic since he was a cradle Catholic. It was easy to change religions again. I never felt there was one right one. I believe there is one God that all religions pray to, whatever that may look like.

Our first year of marriage was not what I had hoped for. Although my husband did love me, he was emotionally unavailable. It took me by surprise that he couldn't show up for me. I was ready to relax and recover with him, but it didn't happen that way.

He was married to staying busy and working and being gone. After work, he would go to the bar with his boss each night. I would have dinner ready and want to eat as a family. It got old really fast when I had to get mad to get him to come home. The bar life was for singles, and I needed to bond with him as a family. My daughter was sixteen, and fighting for him to come home from the bar every night wasn't the kind of example I wanted her to learn. With the high stress of my work, working alone most days, and fighting with him each night, I found myself in deep depression.

I went to my head nurse in October of 1998 and told her I needed to take a leave of absence due to depression. I contacted my doctor, and she said she would sign the form. I needed some time to figure out how to be married to a man who didn't have a clue how to be emotionally available or even show up. We had only been married seven months at that time.

I took twelve weeks off and entered an eight-hour-a-day intensive therapy group for eight weeks in hopes of finding some answers and learning how to navigate a new problem in my life. I figured if I were going to pay the kind of money I was paying for this, I would fight with all I had for my healing and find answers.

The first week, I had a dream that is still as vivid today as then. I saw myself at different stages in my life. First, I was an infant wearing a red football helmet. I was lying on my parents' bed and rolled down to the end of the bed with the helmet on as my dad watched TV and my mother read a book.

I walked by as an adult in a white uniform and saw myself at the foot of the bed, about to fall off. I quickly grabbed myself and cradled myself in my arms, saying, "Oh, you poor thing, you almost fell off the bed! But I've got you now. Why do you have a red football helmet on?" I gently took the helmet off the baby and told her she wouldn't need this anymore, that she was safe, that she was loved deeply, and I would take very good care of her from now on.

I saw myself as an elementary child and an adolescent, and each time, my adult version loved, hugged, and talked softly to each of them. I reassured each version of myself that I was a very special girl and that I didn't deserve the trauma I had experienced. I was embracing and genuinely feeling loved and caressed by myself.

I was showing up for myself. It was a powerful dream, and I knew that was what I had to do from now on. I fought for my healing and left at the end of the eight weeks much more equipped to handle what I had now signed up for.

The red helmet in my dream kept bothering me. Why did my infant-self have it on? I began to pay closer attention to my dreams and dig deep into my soul, trying to find answers and patterns.

I remember being told that my aunt and uncle had raised me for the first few months of life. My mother had a major emergency surgery and required a while to convalesce. My aunt and uncle took me home with them from the hospital. It began to make sense to me that I bonded with them.

When my dad took me back, I felt abandoned by those I had bonded with. I was often told that my older cousin couldn't understand why they had taken his little sister away.

Because I missed out on the bonding time with my own parents, I think this set me up for a pattern I would follow throughout most of life; to accept unemotionally available people.

I started life out with no connection, and my comfort zone was with people who would leave me and not show emotion. From an early age, I knew what it felt like not to feel loved, and I was determined to spend my life preventing as many humans as I could from ever going through that. This is why being a nurse and attending to children's emotional needs was so easy.

When I make a commitment to love, I commit. I don't easily walk away. I believe in love, and we are all worthy of it. I will never be the one who takes it away in life. I know what that feels like, and I would never cause another human to suffer that way. There is always an answer, and I will always find it.

I began to fill my toolbox with this knowledge and knew it would be a long journey, but I was determined to find my healing!

We all have a story.

There's always a reason why we make the choices we make.

I began to dig deeper into why my husband couldn't show up and what he was running away from. He was born the oldest of twelve children. His mother was sixteen when she had him and continued having children almost yearly after him. He remembers washing dirty, poopy diapers out when he was four years old. He looked after his younger siblings as he grew up.

By the time he was eight, he was getting up to milk the cows and slop pigs, which meant waking up at five a.m., going to school afterward, and repeating the chores after school. He lived on a farm that his grandfather had built, which had been in the family for over one hundred and twenty years. He missed out on all the usual, the more normal things other children did.

He was raised in a strict Catholic Church and was taught by the nuns. He was not allowed to talk. He was told you are to be seen and not heard. He got a spanking once for letting a giggle escape during the church service. The nuns would praise him for being an example of the perfect child because he was so quiet and smart. He learned too early in life that his voice didn't matter. All was well as long as he did what he was told and didn't object.

Growing up, he wasn't allowed to have a girlfriend. His mother told him they were trouble. When he was fourteen, he went with his uncle to a house in South Dakota, and there was a girl riding horses who he casually talked to. She wrote him a letter that his mother read aloud as he stood in the middle of the living room floor. He was humiliated and got a big lecture not to mess with girls, only go to school. They demanded he never talk to a girl until he left home.

He missed out on crushes, hand-holding, first kisses, and all the matters of the heart. At seventeen, he was eager to leave home and joined the United States Air Force. The day he got on the bus, he was a virgin in so many ways. His mother told him to keep his pants zipped up at all times. She didn't want any surprises coming back with him.

While serving, he did well and was promoted quickly. He had been used to working hard since he was a child and performed well with policies and procedures. He had been told what to do his whole life, so this was a breeze.

He soared in his career and was promoted to Chief Master Sergeant at a young age because he was a good leader and followed protocol well. His first overseas tour landed him in Labrador, where he met the first girl in his life and married her. They were married for fifteen years. He brought her to America, and they had three children early in their marriage. He provided well, but not at home. He had never been taught what respecting a woman looked like.

He had no idea how to give compliments. He may have thought his wife was beautiful, but she never heard it. Saying "I love you" wasn't something he had heard much in his life.

His parents loved him and were very good people, but they weren't good at expressing love and affection verbally with him. He was the first child, and they were learning.

His first marriage fell apart quickly as he left her in emotional abandonment. In their last year together, he had an affair that broke up the marriage. He divorced his wife and went for his new assignment in Japan six months later. His new lover was also assigned there, and it wasn't long before they married.

His new marriage was tough on his three children and ex-wife. I asked him many times why he didn't fight for that marriage and tried to get out of going to Japan, but he wasn't equipped with the proper emotional tools to do so.

His second marriage was no better. He was jumping from the fire into the fire with no break. Their marriage lasted about twelve years, and they told the same story.

While he was making good impressions on everyone in the service, following orders, and leading others to greatness, his wives were crying in their beers at bars and in someone else's arms.

Professionally, he was the best, and no one could hold a candle to him. Concerning matters of the heart, he was limited and stuck at a child's age. He had been spanked, yelled at, threatened, and defeated while growing up.

Girls and sex talk could wait for adulthood. It was horrible that he couldn't even feel his natural feelings. No hard-ons, no dirty books, no talking with friends about titties, nothing—the exploration of his feelings was taken off the table. He was forbidden to feel and see—talk about a soul jar, and boy, did he have one, and was it packed full! SHAME, FEAR, and GUILT were buried deeply in his jar back to early childhood.

He was extremely handsome, with movie-star looks, and it seemed so sad that such a beautiful soul had been stopped and controlled not to grow emotionally in love. As I learned more about him, I knew he had never been given a chance in life with love. I was deeply in love with him and could feel his deep love for me.

Being the teacher I am and not ever shrinking away from a challenge in life, he became my new mission. I could teach him what respect for women looked like. I could teach him love. I could teach him to feel safe with his feelings. Why should I throw him away just because he was never given the "basic 101 class on respect, love, adoration, and how to feel your feelings"? He would just continue to break hearts and possibly become an alcoholic in the process if I didn't help him.

He had missed out, but I could teach him because I loved him. As long as he was teachable and willing, I'd go to the ends of the earth for him. I began my twenty-six-year journey to try to undo the horrible dysfunctional habits he had learned in life regarding love.

I remember the first time I met his family. I noticed his mother looked awkward when greeting him. She shook his hand and looked embarrassed as she said, "Good to see you."

I hugged her and extended my love and greetings as I was introduced. This was normal for me. I asked him later why he didn't hug his mother. He said, "I don't know, I don't think we do that."

I then asked, "Does she say she loves you?"

He said, "No, we don't say that either."

As I got to know her, I always told her I loved her. She began to say it to him, too. I remember witnessing the first time she hugged him. I asked him later how that felt; he said, "Good." I never knew I had missed that.

There were a lot of lessons yet to be learned. It would be a difficult journey, but I wasn't going anywhere. Time was on our side.

Chapter 24

After my leave of absence was up, I talked to my head nurse about returning to work. I was exhausted, and all of life's stresses had caught up with me. My stress at home was unexpected but needed attention. The emotional impact had hit me square in the face! I didn't want to return to the emotional pull of hurting people, making decisions on such a grand scale, and being alone in a dark office anymore.

After twenty years in the Burn Center, I resigned.

I applied for a Mobile Wound Care Nurse job and got it. There was a pilot study to take a large RV-type bus to nursing homes and perform wound care on the patients. We would bring them to our bus, a clinic on wheels, and provide the care they needed. It was considered an outpatient procedure, and Medicare covered it.

There was a doctor, a nurse practitioner, me, and two techs. It was a lot of fun driving around the city doing wound care with friends. We laughed and felt the sunshine, and we all worked well together. I loved it! I did this job for seven months.

My husband's cousin was a priest, and his aunt was a nun, and they traveled through to see us on May 2, 1999. They spent the night, and I fixed a roast dinner for them. We had a lovely visit, and before they left, Father asked us if he could bless our home. We said, "Of course!" We all held hands before the open door as he said a beautiful prayer over our home and marriage. It was another divine event in our lives.

The next day, May 3, 1999, around 4:30 p.m., I noticed an eerie stillness in the dark sky as I walked to my car to leave work. There was a green cast over the darkness. I decided to rush home to ensure the dog, my daughter, and my husband were safe and aware. I had a bad feeling we were getting ready to have some bad weather.

I turned the television on as I entered the house. The weatherman talked about a tornado on the ground that hadn't lifted for twenty miles and was heading for our side of town.

They were telling people to take cover immediately. It was a deadly one.

Before we knew it, the tornado was a mile away and headed straight for us. I grabbed our chihuahua and a large blanket as my husband, daughter, and I squeezed into the bathtub. As we passed the front door, my husband and I saw debris flying across the street. He slammed the door and locked it.

My husband was praying the Hail Mary. I commanded the winds to leave us alone, and my daughter screamed as she prayed. We all felt sure this would be how we died as we braced for the impact. All of a sudden, it sounded like a train was flying over our house. It also sounded like going down under Niagara Falls and hearing the tremendous roar of water.

There was a tightness in the house. Then we heard glass breaking, smelled the dirt, heard boards snapping, and heard a house next door crumble as we waited for our fate. It only lasted a couple of minutes, and then it got quiet.

In shock that we were alive and well, we made our way out of the tub. The front windows were blown out, and the roof had about five holes, but our house was still standing!

We walked outside to what was once a mature and beautiful neighborhood, to a bunch of sticks where beautiful elms once stood. Houses all around us were flattened to the foundation. There was a boat on the top of a stripped tree. Sheet metal was intertwined all through the branches of what was left of other trees. We even saw Mother Nature's humor. A sign for a house for rent landed in a standing window while the foundation was all that was left.

We checked on our neighbors. Two houses down from us, a couple was found buried in their closet dead. Behind us, a lady had just gotten home and was trying to get inside when she was picked up by the force and thrown into the street dead.

We were the only house for blocks—a mile away north of us—still standing. Houses were reduced to mere sticks. People's belongings were gone, blown somewhere else.

Aside from the blown-out windows, not a single picture, tea cup, or teapot was touched; not one thing was broken in our house full of antiques. My husband had just picked up the mail before the storm hit and had laid it on a brick semi-wall in the breezeway. Miraculously, it still sat there after the windows were blown out. It didn't seem real that so much destruction was all around us, and everything was in its place inside my house.

My daughter's bedroom, which is on the front of the house, took a direct hit. The window was blown out, and the room was full of debris.

One of our friends appeared and began to pull closet doors off and nail them to the windows. He got a large tarp on our roof. Many airmen from the nearby Air Force base appeared to assist.

We began to walk the streets to see the damage done. Everyone looked like zombies walking in circles, not knowing what to do. There were flashing emergency lights everywhere as animals ran and tried to find their homes. It was a sad and shocking sight.

The National Weather Service rated the tornado an F5. It turned out that this deadly tornado stayed on the ground for thirty-eight miles without lifting and killed many in its pathway.

My daughter and I had been to the Federal Building after Timothy McVeigh bombed it in 1995. This looked very similar to that site where everything had just exploded. It's another sight that is so graphic that it's hard to describe.

We slept in our home that night without electricity, but it wasn't safe. Everyone was allowed to take what they could, but no one was allowed to stay. There were too many hazardous materials, gas leaks, and fallen lines. Our dear friends loaned us their travel trailer, which we stayed in for a week. It was impossible to get hotel rooms or a place to rent because the tornado made so many people homeless.

A lovely couple from the church in a part of our neighborhood with less damage invited us to live with them until we could rebuild. They were another God-send.

I could only take a week off from work and continued with my daily job. I was depressed. Losing our home had been the final straw for me. I worked until July of that year.

While driving to work one day, I passed all the sticks that were once beautiful homes. The rubble had piled up and would take months to demolish and remove.

As I drove through all the rubble, I said aloud, "What the Hell am I doing? I'm as broken as all these sticks, and here I am, taking care of other people! I can't do it one more day! I can't take care of one more person. I need to take care of myself!"

I drove to the mobile clinic and told the nurse practitioner they would have to carry on without me because I was incapable of working one more day.

I then drove to our office, emptied my desk, and wrote my letter of resignation, apologizing for not being able to fulfill any more of my duties. Life had thrown too much at me this time. I quit! I was broken and in deep despair.

I checked myself into the psych unit at a local hospital. I couldn't go one more day. I wanted to die. I needed help!

I spent a long weekend in the psych unit resting. After a long talk with the doctor, she told me my feelings were perfectly normal. I was reacting to a traumatic event, and she felt I would benefit most with time away from the horrible site. She exempted me from having to go to group therapy and told them just to let me rest. I appreciated her hearing me and helping me feel like I wasn't going crazy.

It was time for me to rest in life! It was time to heal from all the bad names people labeled me with as a young lady. It was time to release the fear of hearing gunshots while people hated me so much they wanted me dead. It was time to release the voices that said I was not a good mother. It was time to release all the grief I carried as I said goodbye to so many humans.

It was time to feel all the graphic and horrible ways I hurt people for them to heal in the Burn Center. I would no longer have to relive the fingers, ears, and noses falling off in my hands as I apologized profusely while gently medicating their wounds anymore. The real-life nightmare would only torment me in my dreams for a while.

And it was time for me to deal with and heal from the disappointment that my husband did not know how to show up.

Chapter 25

After the tornado, we lived only a few blocks away from our home. I would take a walk every day with our chihuahua, Tony, and sit in what was left of our backyard and just think. Big trucks were busy removing debris and demolishing houses. Within a month, it almost looked like we lived in the country.

One day, as I was sitting in my yard, just staring and thinking, it occurred to me that I had not heard a bird, seen a spider, an ant, or any living thing there since the tornado. The grass blades were ripped off and seemed stunted. I started crawling around, looking everywhere for anything that would move. I crawled all over the yard. Not one living thing was left; everything had been blown away.

Every day for months, I would search. I dug in the dirt; there were no ants!

I was sad that all the happy creatures had also lost their livelihood and homes. Where did they go? How were they coping with all the losses they had seen and experienced? It might have been too much force for their infinite tiny bodies. Maybe they just exploded.

I had a lot of time to think about a lot of things.

During that time, my whole perspective on life changed. I developed a new respect for all living creatures. I decided that all living things mattered, and I would never intentionally kill another crawly thing again.

One of my lifelong fears was spiders. As I sat each day, I longed for the spider to return. I longed to hear a cardinal chirp. Where were my squirrel friends, the possums, raccoons, rats, feral cats, and dogs? Had they all been blown away?

I was seeing God through different eyes, too. I don't think He was mad at anyone the day of the horrendous winds. I don't think He was punishing anyone, either. A lot of people blame Him when things go wrong, but we are all going to die. Some die in more dramatic and tragic ways than others.

It's sad, but it is part of living on Earth.

Storms happen, life happens, fire happens, people drown, and life can be cruel, but I don't think God is cruel.

All my thoughts about Hell changed during that time, too. In my alone time with nature every day, I became convinced that God was all about Love. God is Love, and Love is really all that matters. As humans, we all want love and thrive better when it is present.

I ceased to believe in Hell that day. I knew the God who created such beauty and tiny creatures loved every single human and creature on this earth. I became convinced Hell did not exist as I had been raised to believe.

God would not send any human to a place of fire. These were the things that dropped in my heart as I sat alone each day. It was a remarkable time of inner growth for me, and I have only been growing with God since.

It became more challenging for me to keep going to church. I was tired of all the rules that had harmed so many dear people, including my husband. Broken rules create judgment, and judgment eventually turns to hate. Where does Love have a chance to flourish and heal when one is so busy judging another? Every time you point a finger at someone in judgment, take note—all your other fingers are pointing back at you!

We are all guilty of making mistakes; some call it sin.

Jesus once told his disciples, who were judging a woman who had had seven husbands in her life, to throw the first stone if they were without sin. No one could throw a stone.

Many beautiful experiences are missed out on when we judge someone for doing life differently than we do. Why does their difference make our way right and their way wrong?

We all matter, no matter how we are boxed up, no matter how light or dark our skin is, or no matter what religion we claim. We are all humans, and all bleed red blood! We all poop, and we all need to eat. Why do we think our way is the only way? God is so much bigger than that! There is so much we don't know about Him.

I had sent my daughter and dog to Las Vegas to spend the summer with my parents. I felt getting my daughter away from the destruction would be better for her. As it turned out, she said it wasn't, and I should have allowed her to experience her world as it caved in, too.

In trying to protect her, I took something away she could have only experienced and grown from had she been allowed to stay. What was done in love hurt her and caused more damage.

What a lesson!

Chapter 26

Control!

That's such a complex emotion to deal with. How can you grow when you have spent a lifetime having your choices removed by others? The only way to grow is to take your power back. Only you can do it for you, and only I can do it for me.

As your feelings arise, pay attention to how you feel. Figure out why that one feeling is a button in your life that, when pushed, causes you to react by controlling everything in your pathway.

Who or what took that power from you?

Your reaction to losing your power causes anger and a feeling of not wanting to go through that again. That's when you try to remember the story, like I did with the red helmet.

We can't change our behavior until we understand what is going on and why. Once you understand why you react and choose the way you do, then you can come up with a plan to reprogram your thinking and choices and eventually live in power.

When a feeling slips out of the soul jar and is harsh, demanding, angry, and wanting to boss everyone around, pay attention to it.

Stop and feel the emotion and search your soul for a pattern of when that emotion shows itself consistently. Be determined to change, and be strong in your own skin to overcome anything!

I am proof that if you fight hard enough, you can change from anything! I believe in change and will be fighting for it until I die.

If I micromanage everything, I am preventing someone else from growing or making a mistake they can learn from on their own. I overprotected my children, especially after my son was kidnapped. There was a hard lesson on balance there.

I walked the house at night praying over my two kids for years after that event. As they slept, I would quietly lay hands on them and pray for God's protection for the rest of their lives. I would go to my son's large bedroom window and hold my hands out to the street, claiming protection and angels upon him and my daughter everywhere they went.

My daughter had bladder issues as a young child, and I hovered everywhere to prevent her from being bullied. I was her homeroom mother at school each year and Sunday school teacher. I would educate the children around her that she had a medical condition that caused her not to be able to hold her pee. She always had changes of clothes in her backpack.

You see, when I thought I was protecting my child out of deep love, I was crippling her not to take ownership, and that would later be an issue.

We had a tumultuous relationship in her late teens and into her twenties. We have to give each other choices and let each one experience the consequences, good or bad.

That is how we grow.

It's tough when a whole family is a controller. My husband, daughter, and I are. We have each experienced events that took our power and voices away, and sometimes, it can be challenging to be around each other because of this.

I take my power back daily. I mostly do it silently in my head now.

Sometimes, when I'm alone in my room, I speak authoritatively to the person or thing that pushed my button. I throw my defeat out the window and reclaim my power by speaking it into existence. "Be Gone! I don't need your assistance in this matter. I am worthy, I am strong, I am powerful without controlling another. I can do this!"

I have often told my husband, "You have to fake it until you make it." That's what I have done. It works; our thoughts are powerhouses. Learn to control them, and they won't control you. Keep at it every day, and growth will come.

I give grace for mistakes as long as you are growing with me.

Chapter 27

When my husband Dean and I got married, it was imperative for me to try to blend our new family together. I wanted his three children to grow closer to their father. I also tried to make them feel completely welcome in my world and feel my love. It was easy for me to love them because of my love for their dad.

I sent them each a Christmas card before we got married. I wanted to ensure they knew I would not threaten their relationship with him. I also wanted them to know that I accepted them right where they were and wanted to grow with them in a relationship, whatever that looked like. They were all grown, so it wasn't like I would be raising them. Their mother was very active in their lives, and I saw they were very protective of her.

His youngest daughter, the mother of our grandchildren, got married right after we got married. I noticed some uneasy feelings toward me from his kids and even my husband when a conversation about being at the wedding with their mom came up.

I did my best to stay neutral and support them. I saw my husband's ex-wife at the wedding and immediately knew they had unfinished business. It showed on both their faces. We were all very uncomfortable. It was the first time he and she had seen each other or spoken since he left for Japan many years earlier.

I embraced her and tried to be as sensitive as I could be that night. Later, he and I talked a lot about the feelings I witnessed and how protective the kids were towards her in my presence.

I had no idea feelings for her still lingered for these two. I was pissed because I was in this situation. I would have never married Dean had I known there were unfinished feelings. It wasn't my fault they didn't stay married, but I felt ambushed by the discomfort I witnessed. I tried to keep things calm for the sake of his kids. They cherished their mother, and I respected that. But how in the hell was I going to fit into this scenario?

I had always lived by the motto and scripture when Jesus said, "Bless your enemies and pray for those who despitefully use you."

Dean's parents still had a strong connection to his ex-wife, and his mother confided in me later that she always had hopes they would reconcile. Some of his family remained devoted to her while not embracing me, which always caused me significant discomfort. I could never bond with them and eventually lost interest after many years of being ignored. They were always a source of conflict for us, and it took him a long time to see how I was treated.

I told his mother it wasn't my fault his first marriage had failed, and many years had passed. I said, "I need you to give me a fair chance because I am his wife now. I will be very good to you and him if you only give me a chance. I refuse to live in someone else's shadow." My mother-in-law and I became good friends after that, and I felt loved by her.

I learned to bless my enemies a long time ago. It was how I took my power back for years. Anytime I felt a little hate try to creep into my heart, I quickly took notice and began to pray a blessing over that person or situation. It has always worked. His ex-wife was now my enemy only because the unfinished business represented a threat to my marriage.

I began to pray God would bless her with the best in life. I prayed for her every day until the fear and anger went away. It wasn't long before I felt a love growing in my heart for her. I had taken my power back by facing the threat head-on with positivity. I now felt love where jealousy and anger had tried hard to take residence. I learned to love her on purpose for the sake of their children and myself. I didn't want to cause them any more sadness or grief in life because I couldn't handle my own issues.

It was around 2005 that I got a phone call from his oldest daughter one evening. She said, "Debbie, Mom is in the ICU, and they think she may die. She had a bowel obstruction, and it perforated." She was crying and told me they were scared.

I told her I would get the first flight out and be there in the early morning. I flew into Virginia, and our son-in-law picked me up. We went straight to the hospital. I sat in vigil with them while their mother was critically ill for days.

The first night, both daughters and I stayed in the ICU waiting room, talking all night and checking in on her. It broke my heart for each of my husband's children as I watched them silently stare in horror at the sight of their critically ill mother.

His daughter had given birth to another grandchild I hadn't seen in a couple of years. He was three, and I fell in love with him. We held a vigil for their dearly loved mother and grandmother. I would take the kids to the chapel daily and teach them to pray for her. It was a great bonding time for all of us.

She recovered and had a colostomy. I was well versed in that area and taught her to change, empty, and take care of the bag while recovering. She had complained about how much her back ached from being in bed so long and wanted a bath. I gave her a good bath, changed her colostomy bag, and put a basin of warm water on the floor for her to soak her feet in.

As I washed her feet, she said, "Wow, I sure hope Dean realizes what he has in you. I can't believe you are washing my feet and rubbing my back, his ex-wife!"

I knew that what I was doing wasn't the norm. I knew I was intentionally making choices to take power over a situation that wasn't in my power to change. I could only navigate my response with intended choices. I was choosing to love on purpose. It's the quickest road to forgiveness and benefits us all.

I wanted to tell her that Dean knew what he had, but I also knew Dean was still incapable of realizing who he was married to because he had not yet slowed down enough. He had stayed so busy since leaving home at age seventeen, working two to three jobs at a time, going to college, and traveling all over the world. It would be years before he slowed down enough to grow in matters of the heart.

I also didn't want to project more negativity into my marriage by talking to his ex-wife about him. I learned a long time ago, in nursing school, not to talk about a person with someone else until you have had a chance to find out as much information as possible from the source. That lesson kept me from pre-judging someone because of what someone else had said. I have been able to help many patients and people in my life when I refused to label them because of someone else's judgment.

Dean was still incapable of realizing the importance of expressions of love and adoration. It would take many years, a lifetime, and a million tears from my eyes for him to learn.

Has God ever given up on anyone? I say no. Then why should I give up on my husband? He traveled worldwide for the next twenty years and stayed very busy with his job. He missed most of my birthdays and anniversaries.

He would fly off for at least six years, knowing I would age one more year in a few days. There was no celebration ahead of time. He always attended the SHRM conference every year, which was always on my birthday. Of course, I was always angry about it, but he was too involved in his job to see how he was hurting and abusing me.

I found out in our sixth year of marriage he had been unfaithful. I was utterly devastated. When I found out, I sat down and told Dean he had one chance to tell me the truth. If it didn't match what I already knew, the marriage would end immediately.

He admitted the truth. I told him he had to take at least a month off work and get counseling to prove he was willing to change and not repeat this behavior. I also set up several other consequences, and if he was willing to follow everything I had set up, I would work on learning what forgiving him looked like.

I had gone to a divorce attorney when I first found out about his indiscretion. I took all my papers in and talked with her. I fell apart and began to sob. I felt like I was at his funeral. I cried so hard I could barely walk out.

I couldn't give up on him yet. There were many hard years with Dean. In fact, for the next four years, I walked with him day by day. I was furious that he would do this and had a public outburst with him a few times. I was so disappointed in his lack of commitment and ability to love, but I fiercely wanted to believe in him.

I spent hours kneeling at an altar that I had bought. It was at the foot of my bed. I begged for wisdom and knowledge and courage to know how to navigate this time. God gave me the grace and strength every day. I kept hearing Him tell me to live one day at a time, and that's exactly what I did.

My husband was trying to learn to change. He was coming from a lifetime of not knowing how to respect or love properly, and while I certainly didn't allow him to use that as an excuse, I understood the toolbox he was pulling from.

I tried counseling with the employee assistance program from his work. I went to several people trying to find a match. One day, the lady I was talking to dozed off in the middle of my sharing! She let out a big snore and woke herself up! I was so upset! She apologized and said she had taken Benadryl for bad allergies. I shook my head and never went back.

I searched everywhere, even nationwide, for someone to talk to. I even paid one lady $10,000 to counsel me. At the end of the week, she gave me a blanket, dimmed the lights, and thought she was going to coach me into having an orgasm in front of her!

I was done after that!

I was tired of going to people who fell asleep, told me to leave my husband, judged me, or just weren't smart enough. I knew this was my story to live, and many would not agree with how I navigated it. That was none of their business. It was my story and my ending. I took a grief recovery program, which helped give me some new tools.

There would be a long, hard road ahead until my husband slowed down and decided to address his feelings.

Being unfaithful and getting back at Dean was not even a thought for me. I find others attractive, but have never allowed my heart to go there while in marriage. As I have said before, I go all in when I commit.

I began to spend a lot of money while he was going all over the world. I would buy myself everything I could want or need. I started to live without expectations. I wanted to hurt him and make him feel the horrific pain he made me feel, so I spent lots of money.

He traveled at least two weeks out of the month and was deep in work when he was there. I didn't travel with him because it wasn't fun. I'd rather be at home with my dogs than in a hotel alone all day. Besides my five dogs, who were my soul, shopping was the only thing I had.

I began buying and selling antiques and decorating antique stores. I sold goods at the flea market and made enough money to invest in my hobby. I redecorated the house when the urge hit, which was often.

And then, I began periodically holding classes for my husband on how to show up in love and matters of the heart. I would give him affirmations to write hundreds of times. He would have to get up in the morning and write about what he adored and loved about me. I did the same for him. He has many filled notebooks collected from assignments I gave him in the last twenty-six years.

He was always good about listening and trying to change. As I have said before, that kept me in the marriage, along with the fact that I truly loved him.

Chapter 28

Around July 1999, Dean and I were going to a parade downtown. I missed my little dog, Tony, tremendously since I had sent him to Las Vegas after the tornado. I got a feeling there was a dog that I wanted at the flea market, and it was on our way. I asked my husband to go to the market. That feeling was leading me. I said turn to the right and then left.

We soon encountered a man and his child selling puppies on the side of the road. They looked like they could use the money. The first one I held cuddled close to me and kissed me, and I knew she was why I was there. She was a tiny, white ball of fur, and I immediately fell in love with her.

I could tell she felt the same because when I tried to give her back to hold another puppy, she cried for me until I took her again. We were drawn to each other on purpose. She gave me so much love and adoration and became my angel and protector. She loved me as though it was her mission in life, and I believe it was, too.

As I talked to her, she looked at me like a human. She was very intelligent and was a gift from God. I have often told my husband that she was the greatest gift he ever bought for me. She helped bring me out of depression and brought life back into my world of darkness after the tornado.

Before we left, I asked the guy when she was born, and he said May 3rd of that year! The same day as the tornado! Wow! An angel had been born that day, and God had led me straight to her.

The day the tornado threatened our lives, God produced an angel on earth for me to cross paths with a month or so later. She was born and placed on earth just for me. I named her Victoria, but everyone called her "Pretty" most of the time because she was absolutely beautiful. She was a Lhasa-Pom mix. She never left my side for the next sixteen years. I took her everywhere I went.

She followed us to Texas and died at home after a day of laboring. I knew she had lived a long, fulfilling life, and I cried as I watched her health rapidly decline.

The night before she died, I held her and told her how grateful I had always been for her unrelenting love. I reminded her of all our many adventures and thanked her for always having my back. She had fulfilled her mission and went home to the next world, and it was okay. I would see her again someday. I kissed and hugged her so gently as I cried into her fur.

She chose to go when I wasn't present.

We left for church, and when we came home, she had died in the living room. The other three dogs were very somber and respectful of her body.

I held her for a few hours and took her beautiful angelic body to the vet for cremation. It was hard to let her go, and her death broke my heart. She was a true angel, and I honor her by writing only a tidbit of her wonderful life with me.

We had moved back into our rebuilt house a few months after the tornado. I delayed getting Pretty spayed because I wanted her children. She was the most special dog I had ever owned, and I wanted to preserve her lineage. I told my husband I would see if I could find a male to breed her with. I didn't have to find him; he found me.

One day, a red, short-haired chihuahua appeared on my doorstep. I knelt and asked him where he came from. He had an adorable underbite and a precious face.

My Pretty was in heat, so I invited him in. I told her she could marry this guy and produce some kids for me! I put them on my deck, and it didn't take long for Red—as I called the male—to figure out what to do. When he finished, he went to my front door to be let out and disappeared. I thought he was an angel because I had never seen him before.

Almost two months later, and after she had given birth to four beautiful puppies, I found Red staring into my front storm door. I told him he was the father of three boys and one girl. I brought the puppies out, and he inspected each one with a sniff, looked at Pretty, turned around, and left. I never saw him again. I truly think he was an angel.

Her youngest son was very skittish about everything. He seemed scared of life and a little wild. When he was eight weeks old, I had him and the others out front learning to pee. Before I could turn my head, he had caught a small rabbit bigger than him and killed it.

He carried a strong trait of the Coyote. He was a beautiful white dog with a short, sleek coat. We walked about two miles daily, and he constantly circled the pack and looked around. He was one of my favorite dogs, and his name was Dennis, aka Den-Den.

I remember bringing my chihuahua home after the tornado. His name was Tony, and he weighed about seven pounds. He was so mad at me. For months, he refused to look at me, and if he saw me coming down the hallway, he would turn and go the other way. One day, I picked him up for a long overdue conversation.

All of my animals have always had many nicknames. Victoria responded to Pretty, Beautiful Thang, and Mom. Tony responded to Tall Boy, Big and Strong, Tony, and Tony Maroni.

Holding Tony, I said, "Tall Boy, I need to apologize for sending you away and replacing you while you were gone. I can see I hurt you and made you feel unloved. I know the airplane ride was hard on you. I wanted to make your life easier by letting you stay with Grandpa and Grandma for the summer. I realize I shouldn't have done that. Will you please forgive me? I love you so much."

I hugged him tight, and he kissed me. He was fine after that. He needed to know that he still mattered, too!

All creatures and humans carry basic survival needs, and my dog needed to know that he was still important in my life when I had seemingly replaced him.

Chapter 29

We got a phone call in the early 2000s from one of my husband's family members telling us his father had gotten septic from gallbladder surgery. I could tell he sounded very sick, so we went to him.

He was in the ICU in a small town community hospital. When I first saw him, my nursing instincts kicked in as I observed him and his behavior. He was in a chair with Jello, broth, and other liquids he hadn't touched. His fingernails and lips were a bit blue, and he was confused. He was on oxygen with a nasal cannula, and it was on two liters.

I knelt in front of him so I could see his eyes, and I could see a bit of panic there as he struggled to breathe.

I went out to the nurse's desk and told the nurse my father-in-law was in respiratory distress and needed some help. Her response was, "We are giving him oxygen."

I said, "It is not enough. He is struggling, and he will code if something isn't done soon."

"The doctor wasn't concerned when he made rounds," she said.

"I need you to call him now!"

"We don't call the doctor on the weekend for matters like this."

I told her I had seventeen years of experience as an intensive care nurse and knew what I was looking at. "I want to talk to the doctor now!"

She said, "He's going to yell at me and you!"

"I can handle him; call him now!"

She called him and gave me the phone. I explained to the doctor that I was a family member with seventeen years of experience working in the burn intensive care unit and told him the symptoms my father-in-law was having. I asked if they had drawn blood gasses.

He laughed at me and said, "Who do you think you are, asking me a question like that? We don't torture people in this hospital! That is only done in the big hospitals; this guy is seventy-eight years old and an old man! I know he's crashing, but he's old!"

I stopped him immediately. "You need to listen to me right now. We are not ready to say goodbye to this man, and he is not an old man! He needs more oxygen now! If you are not capable of taking care of a respiratory-distressed patient, I suggest you call one of your colleagues, and you had better do it quickly. If he codes, you are in a heap of trouble!"

Less than five minutes later, they had him in an ambulance and had turned his oxygen up to six liters. My father-in-law had pinked up, and his mental status was normal. They immediately transferred him to a hospital in Omaha, where he was placed in an actual intensive care unit and recovered.

The doctor called me back before we left the unit and apologized. He had called a pulmonary doctor in Omaha who told him I was right.

After he was discharged from Omaha, my father- and mother-in-law went to the follow-up visit with the doctor who almost let him die. When they walked in, the doctor looked at them both with a laugh and said, "Well, you can thank your daughter-in-law for saving your life; I was letting you crash!"

They looked at him in shock, got out of their seats, and walked out immediately. They found a new doctor.

I remember sitting with my mother-in-law one day in the cafeteria in Omaha. She was crying as she said, "I pray I die before he does. I just don't want to live without him." She was seventy years old at the time.

Sadly, it came true. A stroke took her life at the age of seventy-six. We were devastated. I offered to do her make-up and went to the funeral home with one of her daughters and another sister-in-law.

When we walked in, they had her lying on a steel table, completely naked, with her arms hanging down toward the floor. There was no sheet to cover her. I immediately asked the funeral director for a sheet. He was upset that I asked. He was an older man who talked very gruffly to us.

I said, "Do you know who we are? We are her family who loved her, and you should have had enough respect for us to cover her naked body before allowing us in to see her!" She would have never wanted any of us to see her naked!

I covered her and lifted her arms, crossing them over her body. I then took a moment and hugged her, remembering her with respect.

The funeral director continued showing no compassion and clearly had no respect for her dead body or us. He was mad that I called him out for this and that I was doing her makeup with my own foundation. She and I had always played around with makeup, and she liked how I made her look. This guy had a reputation for making people look like clowns, and no one wanted that, which is why I volunteered.

It was tough on my father-in-law to lose her, but he had a very long and active life after that. He always had lots of children and grandchildren checking on him. This "old man" was still putting new roofs on his buildings, gardening, driving tractors, and keeping up with his large farmhouse many years later. He had twenty-two more wonderful years on this earth and recently died three months away from his 100th birthday in the care of his youngest daughter.

Chapter 30

My son lived in California for several years and decided to get his degree. He moved back to Oklahoma and went to a university, where he graduated and met his wife.

They decided to get married on a beautiful beach, so my daughter and I flew to watch this beautiful and exciting event. I was thrilled my son had found the love of his life to settle down with. It was heart-touching to observe the love in my son's eyes as he honored his wife, and they became one. I was so proud of him!

A quick flash of his life raced before my eyes, and my heart soared with love and tears as I witnessed him take this beautiful next step in life. I watched as she walked by me in her gorgeous dress and said quietly to myself, "There's the mother of my future grandchildren."

I beamed with pride as I tried to envision what they would look like. They would be perfect and breathtakingly beautiful to me, no matter what!

A couple of days before we left for Belize, Tony got sick. I took him to the vet, expecting to pick him up after my job at the antique store that afternoon.

I had only been at work for an hour when the phone rang. It was the veterinarian calling. He said he was sorry, but little Tony was no longer with us.

I said, "What? Where is he? Did my husband pick him up?"

He replied, "No, I'm sorry. Tony had a heart attack. We coded him for over an hour, and I just couldn't get him back."

I was in shock!

I left work to go to Tony and found his little body completely lifeless. He had blood coming out of his nose where they had intubated him, and his sweet tongue was hanging out. I held his lifeless body in my arms as I sobbed and apologized for leaving him. I begged my little buddy to wake up! I just couldn't believe he was gone.

It was truly heartbreaking! Another little angel who had traveled many stresses of life with me was now gone. He was with me through all my single years and would see when my heart could hold no more. He was one of the constants in my life when my son left home. It was a huge loss.

I had grown used to loss in life; I had said goodbye to so many people, animals, expectations, and even a baby. It was during these years that the abortion I got in 1980 came back to haunt me.

The good thing about my husband traveling was that I had a lot of time to think, feel, heal, and process the many feelings and events I had pushed into my soul jar. I got to the point where I enjoyed him leaving. It gave me time alone to process a lot of those feelings. We were both very independent people and made our marriage work the best we could.

I began to cry one day as the impact of taking my baby's life hit me. I was sobbing and retching in deep emotional pain. I thought about my child's soul and wondered if it was a boy or a girl.

I had recently seen the Human Body show that was traveling the country. They showed all the stages from conception to nine months, with actual donors and explained when the heart starts to beat. I had not allowed myself to see anything like this for twenty years.

I saw the nine-week-old fetus in a jar and stared in horror, remembering what I had done. I felt so sad and ashamed. I felt guilty. I felt deep anguish. I felt like I had genuinely failed in life. I felt so mad at myself. I felt so sorry for the fetus and hoped it didn't feel the pain.

I went home and knelt on my altar and cried for hours for the soul of my aborted child. I didn't deserve forgiveness for being incapable and doing such a vile act.

My husband and I went to a Marriage Encounter event for a long weekend. It was a good, refreshing time for both of us. A brilliant priest who spoke well from his heart led the event. You'd never know he wasn't married to a spouse; he understood us so well. It was a powerful weekend. We had a moment of confession, and I felt like this was the perfect time to confess my faults and sins to someone else and see if I could unburden my load a little.

I began to sob as I sat with Father. I told him I had killed my nine-week-old fetus about twenty years ago, and I needed to know how to proceed in life with the recent feelings of this horrible burden.

This time, I unscrewed the lid from my jar and allowed all the feelings I had carried way too long to be seen, heard, and validated.

I sat in all the horror and shame of what I had done as the Father compassionately listened. His response was wise and heartfelt.

In the Bible, James told us to confess your faults to one another and pray for one another that you may be healed.

I went home and wrote a letter to my little baby. I named the baby Alex, which would fit a boy or a girl. I allowed space in my heart, soul, and thoughts for this child. I asked Alex to forgive Mom for not being strong enough in life to allow it to come to earth. I honored Alex and could feel a burden lift that I had carried way too long.

I forgave myself.

Chapter 31

I always sought ways to pull my husband and me closer together. The NBA team came to Oklahoma City, so I got season tickets for us. We spent four years enjoying time together, watching our team play. It was just us and perfect date nights. There was always a basketball game on New Year's Eve. We would walk with the crowd to watch the ball drop for a few years. It was a good bonding time.

We'd go to dinner and the movies every week when the NBA season ended. We had a lot of fun times together and were always trying to get closer. Neither one of us ever gave up on each other.

One of the things I love about my husband is he always takes time to admire my creations with me. I love to create beauty in my home and my gardens, and he is good about leaving what he might be doing to inspect my handiwork, making me feel seen and loved by him.

I've had to learn to see his love for me by looking outside the box of life. He may not be the best communicator, but he does make up for it in other ways. I learned to look and live outside the box long ago, and that's where I live with him. It fits in well with my creative spirit.

We are both drawn to beauty; he has a good eye for it, so I appreciate his comments. We both carry a strong spiritual connection, too. We love God and connect on a soul level. We both love our families, and we both want to be married to each other. We have tried hard to find peace in life.

We both are people pleasers and didn't start the marriage out with good boundaries in life. As a result, there's always been someone we allowed in who took our time away from each other. It took several years and a few traumatic events for us to learn what healthy boundaries looked like. Learning to say no was a lesson that would require lots of repetition.

My son called me one day with so much happiness and excitement. "We're having twins, and we have a boy and a girl!" he exclaimed. I felt more happiness than I had ever remembered!

Wow! Twins! My life was about to change big time! We were all so very excited and couldn't wait to meet these beautiful new souls!

My parents had left Las Vegas and moved to Phoenix with my brother. They had all lived together for a while.

I was talking to my dad one day on the phone, and he told me my brother came to him recently and said they had one week to move because their house was in foreclosure. He was shocked because he had been giving money to pay the rent and bills each month to my brother. They didn't know what they were going to do. They had depleted their bank account and couldn't even afford to move.

Apparently, the money was used for something else.

I was so upset that my brother would put them in this situation. This had happened a lot in their life with him. They lost all their life savings over the years because of his choices because they always rescued him.

He and his wife lived with my parents for most of their adult lives off and on. My father was devastated as he told me the story. I told him we would help. There was a rental house next door to me, and I set it up so they could move into it.

We paid for the move and the first month's rent and deposit. My parents lost most of their furniture because my brother had put it in a storage unit and not paid the rent. It gave my mother and I a lot of time together to find new things to make their house a beautiful home. My mother and I bonded in a way we had never done before.

We had four years of laughter, fun, adventures, trips, and trust. I learned to understand my mother's personality better during this time. It was a great bonding time with them both.

I took my dad to all his doctor appointments and physical therapy. He told me stories of his life, and we all got very close, seeing a side of each other we'd not yet seen.

They moved in the same day I got the call that my daughter-in-law was in labor.

We were going to have some babies!

I was elated, and Dean and I drove as fast as we could to Dallas to see our new angels on July 3rd! I was beyond ecstatic. Holding my new grandbabies was the most fulfilling thing I have ever experienced.

There is nothing like watching your kid become a parent!

A few days after their birth, we learned that our grandson had Down's Syndrome. Everyone was shocked, and no one knew this was coming. It took a minute to process, but everyone accepted it. One thing I always respected about my son and his wife was their choice not to treat him differently or baby him too much. He was treated with almost the exact expectations of his sister. He did well.

I began to spend a lot of time in Texas. I spent the first two weeks with them when the babies came home, taking the night shift. I loved being grandma to them and loved being with them! It was a beautiful bonding experience as I would hold and sing to them in the middle of the night.

As I held their precious bodies, I would pray for their life ahead, for God's protection, favor, and blessings to always be with them.

Leaving so often puts more of a strain on my marriage because when my husband wasn't traveling, I was in Texas so that he could stay with our five dogs and parents. We saw each other very little over the next four years. I spent almost as much time in Texas as in Oklahoma.

I'd bring the twins to our house for a couple of weeks at a time, as often as their parents would allow. My husband and I loved being grandparents and having them around! It definitely is a great youth serum! Nothing can make you feel and act younger than young children!

To me, there is nothing more precious than a child. I love to hear them laugh, talk, sing, and learn in their innocence. They are indeed God's angels!

I remember driving home to Oklahoma early after the twins were born. All of a sudden, I began to cry and had to pull over. I started to sob so hard it felt like I was pulling the tears from the depths of my toes. After sobbing for a good fifteen minutes, I began to say thank you over and over for another fifteen minutes.

I realized why I was still here and why God had let me continue to live all the times I wanted to give up. There were so many dark times throughout my ventures in life that I just wanted to give up and couldn't figure out why I was still here.

I had dark days after my divorce from Donny when I wanted to die. Early on during my marriage to Dean, all I could see was darkness. I had to learn how to pull myself up out of the depths of despair by myself. There were times when all I had was a broken string to pull myself up out of the darkness with, but I always did it! I had to teach myself how to heal.

So many others failed me, and I could blame them or look inside to see what I could do differently. I was so glad at that moment that I had hung in there and survived the dark days!

I was also profoundly thankful that I kept and raised my son. Look at what he had given me thirty-five years later! I can't imagine missing out on this in life.

Sometimes, life is so dark, and we wonder why we have been created to suffer so much. We bring most of our suffering to us by our choices in life. We get stuck at some level. Until we decide to move on and help ourselves without pointing fingers at others, we remain stuck and depressed.

I was all I had for so long, besides God, that I had to figure out how to navigate my life. I learned to depend on myself and make choices that caused growth. Growth is painful! My attitude has always been I'd rather feel the pain now than stay stuck and not grow.

I wouldn't have ever wanted to miss getting to know these two bundles of joy! Little did I know two more beautiful angels would be added to the bunch in a few years!

They were two of the most beautiful souls God had ever created, and I believe he made me to be their Grandma! It truly changed my life! I had never been happier. I knew I was supposed to be in their life to teach them, love them, and help them become the beautiful souls they came here to be!

I was so very grateful that I could be there and accepted it with Honor! Every single moment I ever spent with them was indeed a golden experience for me and them.

I loved to engage them. I loved taking them places and sharing life with them. I loved just sitting with them and reading or telling them a story! I loved their laughter! I had once again found my calling in life, being their grandma!

The next twelve years with my grandchildren would be the greatest investment I would ever make, and I did it with pure joy, love, happiness, and intention.

My granddaughter would ask me to tell them a story, and I often made up stories on the drive home to Dallas about animals we'd see in the fields. The twins were easily entertained. As I drove, I would tell them about the recent special meeting the cows had called. It seemed the farmers were wanting to bottle their farts to help with the environment, creating a new fuel option. The cows had heard that it could save them from dying so young and becoming hamburgers. All the lead cows held a class teaching the herd how to make the biggest and loudest farts. They had found that eating certain grasses could create the best farts, and swishing their tail six times counterclockwise would make the fart last longer!

That would always make them laugh long and hard. Soon, they were making up their own stories. We had a very special bond. Our times together were always filled with laughter and fun!

OK. Back to my parents and the move.

I got my parents all moved in and helped them get furniture. I loved having them next door. I loved spending time with them and getting to know them as adults at this stage. We'd play cards together and would eat together daily.

My dad had been limping a lot, and it was getting worse. He was also having trouble with his left arm and neck. I had bought him a motorized scooter to use in public. They had been there less than a year when he got diagnosed with amyotrophic muscular disease, aka ALS.

I was very sad to hear that he would die of such a horrible disease. He was one of the lucky ones; his progression was slow, and he lived another eleven years, never lost his speech, and never had to go on the ventilator.

I was thankful I was next door to help him and my mother. My husband and I spent the next four years helping my parents.

We put our needs on hold while we helped care for them. I was also going back and forth to Texas about every two weeks.

My father was very demanding, and when he wanted something, he wanted it yesterday. He was impatient and couldn't give you five minutes to arrive. He was angry and yelling if you didn't jump the moment he said jump!

It was very frustrating and extremely stressful. Sometimes, my dad would call late into the night to help my mother and I would be asleep. He would be complaining if I took too long to wake up and get there. I would tell him he needed to be more patient and give us a chance to get our shoes on or finish whatever we were doing, but it never mattered. It seemed we were there to serve him!

I had taken part of the fence down in the backyard to make it easier to get to them faster. In essence, I took our boundaries down!

Once, when I was in Texas, my husband had arranged to take my father to the doctor. My husband's office was only about five minutes from our home. He had been on a call that lasted longer than he had planned. He rushed out of his office and sped home to get my dad. As he pulled onto our street, my parents left in their van. My mother was driving; they saw him and kept going. There was no consideration for my husband's job or his feelings.

The control and manipulation we allowed them to have over us was awful. They would get mad at me for going to Texas so often and manipulate me into feeling like I was doing something wrong by wanting to spend so much time with my family there. It was a constant mind battle, and the stress was unreal.

Neither one of them needed constant care at that time. My father could still transfer himself from his chair to the scooter. He also could get in and out of bed with my mother's help and feed himself. They were never without my husband or me.

There was always so much jealousy with my parents. They would get jealous if I spent my time anywhere other than next door with them. The good times came with a price—we were never fast enough. We both gained weight and had chest pain because we were always jumping.

Part of my father's demands was his personality, and part was how he dealt with his loss of independence and autonomy. I felt terrible that he had to deal with the loss of walking and other things. It broke my heart as he was always active and alive.

I would talk to him about his loss periodically. He would tell me how sad he was that he couldn't trim the rose bushes anymore. I understood his feelings and his loss of control in his world.

He had never been patient with nurses whenever my mother was in the hospital. He expected them to drop their world if she needed help. If she needed a pain shot, he would raise a lot of hell to get it for her. She had arthritis and had back issues her whole life.

I began to educate him on how to treat people to help him to be more patient. He did get better, and I was always thankful I was there to diffuse any situation I knew could turn volatile.

I tried to tell him he had to stop being so demanding because we were living in a time when people didn't put up with that anymore. He had no problem cussing someone out or threatening to slap them.

Taking the fence down was something I should have never done. It represented so much concerning personal and inner boundaries in our lives. It became an open door on both sides. It appeared nothing was sacred anymore.

I welcomed my trips to Texas to be with my beautiful family and to get away from the stress of not doing things right at home with them. I loved them so much and wanted to help them when they needed me. I felt like I owed them for how much they had helped me and my son earlier in life. There wasn't anything I wouldn't do for them, and God knows I did it all.

The fact was, my husband and I were getting tired of jumping so high and having no control over our own lives.

Chapter 32

On Easter morning, 2012, I was watering my flowers in front and saw my parents pull in with my brother and his wife. Somehow, I knew what that meant. My brother needed something and had returned to get it from them. He would be moving in again.

I had heard them complain so much about how he had used them and how nice it was to save some money again. They were finally in a spot where they weren't being used for ulterior motives or money and seemed happy.

It angered me that a sight I had witnessed or been told about by my parents for decades was repeating itself right before me! All their conversations about him came rolling into my head while I remembered all they had lost because of him.

I lost it. I couldn't keep my outrage any longer and angrily confronted my brother about returning to take more from them. We exchanged heated words, and I called his wife a name. He then body slammed me and began to choke me, telling me to stop talking about his wife like that! I ripped his shirt off, and he finally let me go.

My dad witnessed the whole thing and did nothing to help me. He didn't care that his son was choking me. My dad told my brother to get in the house. They both went in and closed the door on me.

I was furious! In one moment, my parents had chosen their son over me again and discounted all I had done for them the last four years. I had been caring for them night and day for years, jumping through hoops without notice, forsaking my own health and well-being to make my parents happy, comfortable, and safe.

Being choked was traumatizing enough, but more so, my dad not telling my brother to get off of me. It was impossible to process. I sat on the experience for a few days. My parents didn't reach out. There was silence next door for the first time in four years; their son was back, and they didn't need me. They didn't even think they needed to check on me.

I realized I had been used and not appreciated. I came in with no boundaries, and the war erupted. That was a lesson in the making I would soon be learning through other avenues.

My motives for helping them were always about love, safety, and giving back. I cared for my parents because I deeply loved them and did not expect material or monetary things. They had nothing, and I bought them most of what they had. I truly wanted them to be well-cared for, safe, and happy.

My husband and I went to their house the following week to discuss what had happened. I told my father I was so upset that he had allowed his son to disrespect me in the way he did. I was still furious, and I asked him how he could witness any man choking his daughter and not react. It was unfathomable. I told him I was tired of seeing my brother use them and take from them, and he was here to do it again.

"You are choosing to go back into the same fire that burned you many times before. You know this story well, and I can't keep rescuing you guys."

My father's response hit a deeply buried trigger that surprised me. He was apathetic to my concerns and said, "This was none of your business."

"You made it my business when you told me the stories," I replied.

He said I needed to keep my damn mouth shut and leave them alone. He also denied witnessing me being choked. My father's reaction caused me to blow my top. In fact, both he and my mother said my brother didn't choke me.

Memories of his father came rushing into my head. I was a young child, and for years, my grandfather would touch me through my panties on our visits to their home. He would laugh his big, boisterous laugh and tell me I better not tell anyone! He said he would call me a liar and blame it on me if I did!

I told no one for decades. I was scared to death. At the same time, I had a friend who was six years old who would ask me to spend the night. If I didn't perform oral sex on her, she would chase me through her house with butcher knives.

My uncle was also showing me his penis. Then, when I was nineteen, my father and mother had a brief separation, and my sister, son, and I stayed with him.

I was sad one night and cried to my dad. He hugged me, held on too long, and then grabbed my face to kiss me. He planted a long, passionate kiss with his tongue down my throat. I screamed, pushed him away, and ran down the street, crying in shock at what he'd done.

When I came back, nothing was mentioned about it. I buried it deep in my jar, where the other sexual transgressions against me lived.

I grew up in silence about this stuff because I had been told to stay quiet!

After my dad called me a god-damn liar, he leaned forward and tried to slap my face as he so often had done in my life! He couldn't reach me and missed.

The lid of my jar exploded as I looked at him and screamed. "I'm not a liar; you are, and I swore I would take your transgression against me to my grave to protect you, but no more!"

"Now that I'm fifty-six, you can't slap my face anymore. You're in a wheelchair! You can't put your nasty tongue down my throat anymore, either!"

He called me a god-damn liar again and began to cuss me out profusely while saying I was making stuff up. I said, "No, Mister, I am not, and you and your nasty daddy can't molest me anymore, either."

My father said, "You leave my daddy out of this!"

I said, "Nope, he molested me every time we visited them for years! I'm done with lies, staying quiet, and protecting people who don't give a crap about my well-being."

My mother asked me what I was talking about and later chose to believe I was making the kiss up. I said some horrible things to my father, things and frustrations I had carried for years. Things I protected him from while I struggled to find my voice and believe I mattered. I was done protecting those who tried to quiet me!

It was an ugly scene, but one that gave me part of my power back. My father chose to continue to call me a liar, which sealed the doom of our relationship. I was free and not going back to the prison of silence.

He and my mother bought their new home, and my brother moved in with them. My obligation was done! I had helped ungrateful people who had tossed me away so easily. I owed them nothing more in life. They had made their final choice to let him be their caretaker.

It was a dark time for me. I needed to get out of there. I began to go to Texas more and more often.

When I was around my beautiful grandchildren, all I saw and felt was joy, happiness, laughter, and bliss. They were such angels and such a bright light in my very dark world.

I was so disappointed in my parents. They didn't even give us a heads-up that they were considering a move. My husband and I rearranged our lives, schedules, and priorities to accommodate their desires and wants.

We were on call constantly and couldn't do anything without feeling guilty if it didn't include them. They would show their jealousy. We had given them our souls! We were so sad, broken, and depressed. I felt like I needed to get out of there and find a new start.

Before we could look into leaving Oklahoma, another storm hit. There was a tornado nearby, and the sirens were blowing.

Both my husband and I tried to get to my parents to help them get into the storm cellar. In our stress, we had forgotten the code for the garage and couldn't get into the house to help them. We banged on their doors for ten minutes. My husband could see them walking back to their bedroom. I kept trying to call them, but they wouldn't answer. The winds had gotten so bad we had to get in the shelter.

While in the shelter, my mother texted me that she had fallen down the stairs while getting Daddy in the cellar, and her arm was bleeding. I said I would be over as soon as the sirens let up to help them get out. She said, "Don't bother. I have called the fire department, and they are coming to get us out."

I was tired of chasing her and being manipulated, so I let the firefighters rescue her. She told everyone that we didn't even try to help them. She would always twist everything around to look like the victim.

I wouldn't be playing this game anymore.

Chapter 33

My son had been asking us to move to Texas to watch the kids grow up. There's nothing I wanted more. I needed to be around people who were happy and loved me for who I really was. I needed to find peace. My husband and I agreed to move to Texas in 2014. It was a life of pure peace and one that I hadn't experienced in years.

We celebrated everything together, traveled, ate, laughed, and shared deep love with the children. I had never been happier.

I had buried my feelings with my parents for a while to enjoy all the love around me. I had time later in life to deal with all the disappointments and harshness of Oklahoma.

There was another surprise: my grandson was born, and I would be taking care of him! I was so very excited and happy! This grandchild looked just like his dad when he was a baby, and it was such a joy being with him every day.

It would be eleven months later when the next and final angel would come to us!

I have always called them angels because I believe they are. The four of them absolutely changed my world. Each one had their own unique way of doing so. It gave me great joy to watch them pray and talk to me and each other. They never seemed like kids but mini adults with so much life and wisdom in them. They loved me and loved to be at my house. Someone was always staying over, and they would cry when they had to leave.

We were close. I sat with each of my grandkids, and they had my full attention when they were here.

I made them feel seen.

I made them feel heard.

I was tired but happy and loved being Grandma to these four beautiful souls! I loved every single day I was with them. It was the greatest joy of my life! We spent the summers swimming at the community pool, visiting zoos, and staying busy for five years.

I had the youngest two from 6:30 a.m. until around 6 p.m. for years. We stayed busy around the clock, and everyone had an extracurricular activity they were taking. I would pick the twins up after school, take them to school, and then to everyone's activities.

They all took swimming lessons, one had acting and dance camps, one had gymnastics, and two took taekwondo; we were always running, but it was always fun! I loved listening to them engage with each other as I drove.

It was so wonderful to live in such peace and joy. These children were absolutely healers for both my husband and me; they didn't even know it. We both healed so much from all the stress we had lived under just by being in the presence of innocence, laughter, and pure joy!

My sister had gotten a divorce in the early 2000s. Her doctor-husband had become an addict and was prescribing narcotics to dealers. He was sent to prison and died an early death in his 50s after a six-year sentence.

She never finished medical school and went through her third year when she became pregnant with their first boy. She decided she wanted to be a mother more than a doctor. She would have six boys throughout their marriage.

After her divorce, she was penniless. He had spent all the money on drugs, and they lost their beautiful home, farm, and vehicles. It was a sad story, and I felt terrible for her.

I loved my sister and did everything I could to help her.

She had moved to Las Vegas while my parents still lived there. There were many hard and hungry years for her and her boys, but my parents helped her pay her rent and bills.

After my parents bought their house, my sister moved to Oklahoma to help them. My brother lived there but couldn't help like he thought he could. She got a rental house just a few houses away from them and began to help care for my dad as he got worse.

She was in Oklahoma about three years after we had been living in Texas. I found out she was working in Dallas occasionally.

We had been living in peace in Texas, and it was something I didn't want to lose. I told my sister she would be welcome to stay in my home. She just needed to leave the drama in Oklahoma. I didn't want to hear about it or be involved in any way at all.

We were still healing and enjoying a good life with our grandchildren, and I carried a fierce protective spirit over them. I asked her not to talk about my grandkids to anyone there. I didn't want any negativity cast toward my angels, even from afar.

I told my sister I wanted nothing to do with the constant turmoil. My mother found fault with everyone and everything. No one could ever do anything to please or live peacefully around her.

My sister gradually began to vent each time she would come and stay, and before long, she had brought the drama to Texas. I understood what my sister was going through because it matched my stories. I felt bad for her and allowed her to vent to me.

The problem with that was I had shelved my feelings toward my parents. I had done the best thing for me and my husband by leaving, but I hadn't dealt with the constant volatile situation with them yet.

I was enjoying the rest and peace before I could dive into those feelings, which I was in no hurry to address. But my sister's stories triggered my undealt feelings. When you have to walk on eggshells around someone, only continued damage is done. There is no freedom to share your feelings and no sense of safety.

It was impossible to talk with my parents; from my sister's stories, the story between my parents and I had changed. She was telling a different version. As I have said before, we all have a story to tell, and we tell it from our perspective. If the truth is being told, the versions should match up.

I was still carrying a lot of silent stress. In 2017, I had been doing a lot of gardening and just didn't feel good.

I went to watch my granddaughter cheerleading for the football team. As I sat down by my son, I had a look of panic in my eyes. He said, "Are you okay?"

I said, "I don't think so. I'm either having a panic attack or getting ready to have a damn heart attack."

He and I walked away together and talked a bit. It felt good to have his support, but I was sick.

I was anxious and felt like something was getting ready to happen. I couldn't catch a good breath and noticed my color was off. I had a little bit of pressure in my chest, but it was not unbearable.

My daughter and I had stopped by a store, and I caught a glimpse of myself and could tell something was wrong. On the way home, I told her to take me to the ER and drop me off. I told her I just wanted to get checked out, I would call her later, and she could pick me up.

My husband had left town hours earlier to take his oldest daughter, who was visiting, to Nebraska. We gave her our truck, and they would visit relatives on the farm. They had made it to the Kansas state line.

As soon as they did the EKG on me, they placed the oxygen tubing in my nose. The oxygen helped so much. I felt like I had come back to life! I could breathe and relax.

People were running in and out of my room, drawing blood, giving me aspirin, and asking questions. They told me my troponin levels indicated I was having a heart attack. They were rushing me to the cath lab. I made a call to my daughter, and she informed everyone else about what was happening.

I had a minor heart attack that didn't require a stint. The artery involved was a small one and blocked 100%. The doctors said my heart would reroute around it, and I would be fine.

I had spent four days in the heart hospital back in 2013 after the confrontation with my parents in Oklahoma. I was having pressure in my chest, and my labs were out of whack then. During that stay, they discovered I had an aortic root aneurysm measuring 4.3 centimeters.

Trying to escape the stress would be good in many ways. It was important for my health and well-being. I needed to slow down at some point and remember that I mattered. I still had blood coursing through my veins, and I was still alive, but I was still living for others and not myself.

I was thankful I had my grandchildren to help me heal with their laughter and love. They were God's angels to me!

I treasured my dear children and grandchildren. They meant everything to me. They had become my world and purpose. As tired as I was, I was happier than ever being Grandma to four beautiful souls every single day.

I chose to take my power back from a distance with my parents, and as long as I wasn't exposed to the toxicity, I was much happier. I felt free from them. I still loved them both deeply and still do.

I would feel guilty not talking to my mother and tried to reconcile many times, but I was always the whipping post, and I finally realized I wouldn't be able to grow from this codependency if I didn't separate myself from it. I realized I couldn't be around drama anymore in my life. I chose peace and harmony. All I could do now was pray for her and send love-filled texts. I would never stop loving her.

I could see my sister had fewer boundaries than I did, and I talked with my husband about her staying with us.

My sister had told me once that if a woman doesn't take care of her husband, she has no remorse for having an affair with him. She had an affair with a married man once and had said this to his wife as she confronted her. I didn't agree with this concept and was a bit fearful of letting her be alone too much with my husband. After all, we were still working on our marriage, and I was still trying to teach him what intimacy looked like.

I warned my husband to be very careful and aware. I would not be forgiving of any more mistakes! I watched everything and could tell if the opportunity was right; she would not hesitate to take it.

She stayed with us for almost two years while she occasionally worked in Dallas. My home was also a safe place for her to escape when the drama got too much to bear in Oklahoma. I remember her telling me one day that I was living the life she wanted. Something about that didn't settle well with me. I felt she threatened my home and peace, but I kept it in the back of my mind.

The VA had set my dad up with all he needed for his care at home. He was well cared for by them. They gave him 100% disability since he jumped out of airplanes in the Korean War era. With this came a large amount of money my mother could use to hire help. She was paying my sister-in-law at first, then my sister and her boys to help my dad.

I enjoyed my sister's visits. We had never kept in touch during her marriage, and catching up on life was good. I truly loved her deeply and often told her so. Each time she would visit, we would go junking and load her car up to the brim with treasures. I would give her money on every visit. I wanted to relieve her suffering if I could. Since she had colon cancer, I helped her while she was in the hospital. I set up a go-fund-me for her, as she had to take time off work. I did everything I could to make life easier for her. After she healed from the cancer, she focused more on helping my dad.

It had been six years since I talked to or saw my father. I saw my mother at the hospital when my sister was in for cancer, and we were cordial.

Chapter 34

It was September 2019, I had just gotten out of the shower and dressed when my granddaughter brought me the phone. My sister told me my dad wasn't doing well, and he wanted to talk to me. She gave him the phone.

I said," Hello, Daddy."

He cried as he heard my voice and said, "Hello, Debbie. Baby, I'm so sorry. Please forgive me, please forgive me. I was wrong."

I said," It's OK, Daddy, I forgive you. Please forgive me, too. I said a lot of hateful things to you out of anger that I had buried, but I love you, Daddy."

"I know. I love you, too, honey. It's so good to hear your voice. I have missed you so much!"

"Daddy, I have missed you, too. Thank you so much for calling me."

It was a short call but powerful and full of love and forgiveness. My granddaughter was standing there, and as I ended the call. I said, "My daddy is dying." We hugged tightly as she supported me.

My husband was traveling in Afghanistan then, and my daughter was at work. I called my son and told him about the call, and he asked me if I wanted to drive to see him. My son, his wife, the four grandkids, and I went to Oklahoma within the hour.

This phone call had happened because of my sister. She knew my dad had entered the first phase of dying and had asked him if he wanted to talk to me. He said he did. I was so happy my dad had called. I assumed my mother knew we were coming. On the way there, it didn't occur to me that she didn't know. She was cold when she saw us.

I walked into my dad's room and saw a once vibrant man who had become skin and bones. My heart broke as I rushed to him in a deep embrace. When he saw me, he cried and said, "My God, you look just like me! Look at that white hair!"

I said, "Well, I am your daughter."

My dad replied, "Yes, you sure are, baby."

We held each other tight. It felt wonderful to be on good terms with my dear dad on his deathbed. Despite all the troubles, I had never stopped loving him. God had given us one final goodbye. It was truly beautiful.

We only stayed for about an hour, and the reception by my brothers and mother was uncomfortable. My older brother walked into the room as we sat at his bedside and looked at my dad, saying, "I thought we weren't doing this!" as he pointed at me.

I looked at him, trying to diffuse the discomfort, and said that Daddy had called me. It was a very uncomfortable atmosphere. Of course, there would be drama!

It took my dad two weeks before he died. I had gone to see him a few times after my first visit. The second time I visited, I saw that my sister and older brother planned to go to the cemetery to pick out a plot. I asked if I could go. My sister was very cold to me. She acted like she didn't know me the whole time we were there. I thought it was odd since we had been so close and spent so much time together.

When we were at the cemetery, my brother began to tell me what an awful person I was for talking to our dad the way I did. He told me I was bipolar, too. I told him, first of all, I am not bipolar, and he isn't a psychiatrist to give me that diagnosis. I also told him to stop saying that to me because it wasn't true.

He had heard that I had started taking an antidepressant after my second divorce. It seemed a lot of people thought a person could not be normal if they were on an antidepressant—the stigma of mental illness.

From that moment on, he called me bipolar. I chose not to engage all the other years but stood up for myself this time. He said it so often I asked my psychiatrist if I was bipolar, and she said absolutely not. She was a respected doctor and knew me well over the years in the Burn Center. She saw me all over the hospital with the wound care team. She had more to go on than just a ten-minute office visit.

She said, "Don't listen to people who say those things to you! You have been through so much; you just need a little help to get you to the next step in life with the antidepressant."

I told him he was repeating something he had not witnessed and that there was always more to the story. I also asked him to please stop slandering my name. Everywhere he went, he would tell people what an awful human I was, and they chose to accept that and sit in judgment.

He said I would never think of cussing my parents out like you did! I said, "Oh really? Have you forgotten the first twenty years after you left home, you were always calling home and cussing out our mother? Daddy would get on the phone and cuss you out, telling you not to talk to his wife like that! I witnessed it many times."

"That's not true!"

The truth is my brother and his wife spent twenty years angry at our parents and were always fighting with them. My heart was always sad about it. My brother had reason to be mad at them, and he was just trying to deal with all the lies of his adoption. He had a lot of anger and feelings. I'm sure he was trying to process his life growing up.

It's easy to throw stones when you judge someone else, and he was throwing boulders at me.

On my last visit with my dad, my sister asked me to help her change his dressing and bedding before my husband and I left. My mother and brother were hovering over us. They didn't want me involved in my father's care. I only changed him once, helping put a dressing on his bedsore, and leaving after that. They were so uncomfortable. My brother came in the room and yelled at us, demanding we do this and that and turn him to heal his bedsore!

I gently said, "Hospice is comfort care, not healing care. Daddy is dying and needs to be as comfortable as possible now."

They both flew off the handle, accusing me of coming back and taking over.

After my sister and I got my dad comfortable, I looked at my father and said, "Daddy, I love you, and I am so glad you called me. I didn't come back here to fight with anyone, and I won't be back. I love you so much. I'll see you on the other side." I hugged him and kissed him goodbye for the final time.

My mother said, "Come on. Why do you have to leave mad? Let's talk about this!"

I hugged my mother and told her I loved her and was not mad, but no one would pull me back into this drama and yell at me.

She called me the next day, accusing me of making my dad's bedsore worse! She said it was black now since I had treated it! I told her that was ridiculous and he was dying. She was trying hard to blame me and wouldn't let it go.

I allowed myself to get into a yelling match on the phone as she pulled many things out, creating the drama she was most comfortable in. I finally hung up and decided it was best not to answer any more calls. She could create drama faster than anyone I had ever met. I never understood why she couldn't be happy and at peace with everyone at once. Drama was her comfort zone in life; we all have one.

My sister called me on September 19th and said he had passed in his sleep. I told her I loved her, was sorry for her loss, and thanked her for caring for him so well. I hung up and tried to call my mother, but she didn't answer. I tried several times later and never got her.

That was it. My dad was dead, and I had no relatives to talk to about him.

They were there; I was here, alone. What do I do now? What do I do with all these memories flooding my heart? I longed for my family to share and talk about those memories.

I called my sister back and asked what was going on. She told me they had been there to remove his body, and there would be a five-minute ceremony at the military cemetery in a few days. That was the last time my sister was friendly to me for some reason. I thought at the time it was grief; maybe it was. She had become friends with my brother, and he hated me. She could no longer be my friend and his, so she made a choice.

It was so hard for me to sit still. My dad was dead, and I needed someone to talk to about him. I needed to be around someone who knew and loved him. I wanted to celebrate his life. I wanted to talk to my son and talk about his memories, but he was quiet and didn't want to talk. My husband was there but didn't talk about it; I needed to talk about it. My daughter gave her silent support.

I drove to Oklahoma to hug my mother and try to give her support. I told her I would pay for a service in the funeral home so we could get together as a family. I told her I needed to be around my family. He was my father, too, and I needed a place to gather.

She told me I would have to clear it with both my brothers. I called my older brother and told him I would like to pay for a service at the funeral home so we could gather as a family with music, say goodbye, and then have the service at the cemetery afterward. I wanted to eulogize my father.

He screamed at me and told me if I did that, he would not be there and he would pull the military service!

After he screamed at me, I hung up. My mother called my other brother and told him what I wanted.

He screamed, and I could hear every word he said, "Momma, Debbie is trying to come here and take over again! No! We're not doing that! I'm almost there; I'll handle her when I get there!"

I told my mother I needed a family gathering to say goodbye to him. It doesn't have to be a long, drawn-out affair. My sister-in-law said, "Debbie, we have already done that. We had a service around Daddy's bedside, and everyone sang and said their goodbyes while he was alive."

I was shocked! They had completely left me out! They were all mad that my dad chose to ask for forgiveness by calling me on his deathbed, and they were sitting in judgment against me.

After I heard my brother screaming that he would be there soon, I told my mother I was leaving. I looked her in the eyes and told her I loved her deeply and wished I could be there to support her. I also told her what a wonderful wife and caretaker she had been to him, and my heart hurt so much for her loss of sixty-six years.

She said, "Why do you have to leave? Your brother will be here in a minute. Let's all just sit down and talk!"

I said, "No, I heard every word he said. He doesn't get to yell at me anymore! The last time I saw him, he had his hands around my throat! I love you, but I'm leaving."

I was shaking as I left, partly because I didn't want another run-in with my brother. The other part was the shock of how very dysfunctional we all were as a family. I had never heard of or met anyone more dysfunctional. No one could put aside their drama long enough to come together for one hour and bury their father. They all thought I was Satan's wife because I stood up to my father about the sexual abuse from him and his father.

No one would ever know how much courage it took to pull that out and stick to my guns when he vehemently called me a damn liar! Every time I would try to talk to my mother, the story got bigger and worse over time about what was said the night that I confronted my dad. She had embellished the situation for so long that she didn't even remember the truth. I was shocked at what my sister had told me but not surprised.

I drove home and realized I was better off without these people in my life. Even though I would always carry a deep love for them as my siblings and mother, I didn't deserve that kind of treatment. At some point, I had to acknowledge in life that I mattered!

I went home, crawled into my bed, and played old church music that reminded me of my father. I sobbed for hours as I remembered my father all alone. I remember a moment of sobbing, and I felt a hand on my shoulder. I slowly turned around, thinking it was my husband, but no one was there. The hand lifted as I turned back. It was my father. He could see everything now as it really was. He knew how much I loved him and was there to comfort me. I will never forget how it made me feel. I could feel his presence for days.

I talked to him and thanked him for a good life. He was the glue to our family. He was the reasonable one. He had flaws, but don't we all?

The day before the ceremony, I decided I needed to go. My husband, daughter, and I got dressed and began the drive. I was in the back seat, and as we got about an hour from the cemetery, a heaviness came over me. I asked them to turn off the radio, and please pray for me. I told them I wasn't feeling good. I didn't think I could do this. They began to pray the rosary.

We got to the cemetery, and I saw my sister drive up behind us. She hadn't talked to me since I called her after my dad died. Relatives went to her car and hugged her. No one came to our car. I was starting to feel a panic attack coming.

When everyone got out of the vehicles, my mother and brother were together, and my sister went to sit down. My older brother asked me if I wanted to join the family, and I said no.

It was too late then. I couldn't sit still and pretend for others.

I had been alone in my grief for days while they comforted each other in their dysfunctional ways. I lost it and let out a loud scream that woke up the dead, saying I can't stand to be here. It all seemed so hypocritical. I ran to the car to leave and then went running back to the grave while my mother, brother, and sister were walking out holding the flag.

Without thinking, I said, "My name is Debra Jean, and I am my father's firstborn child! I loved my father, and he loved me. My tears matter! I matter! You people left me out! I matter!"

My mother frantically said, "Oh my God, get her out of here!"

My brother told my husband he better get me out of there. I shot a few of them the finger as we left.

We drove back to Texas pretty much in silence. Emotional support was still my husband's weakness. I had so many beautiful memories flooding my soul and just needed someone. I remembered the good times, not on purpose; they were just there. My dad and I had forgiven each other, and I had let go of the abuse.

My family and extended family were all sitting in judgment over hearsay. They had all taken sides, and it wasn't mine. Isn't that the way it is in life? People blame the victim.

The victim isn't supposed to speak out or show their reaction to the abuse or crime. All we ever see are how stoic people are while they bury their feelings away. The difference in being stoic here publicly with me was no support. It's easy to hide your emotions from the public when you have someone in private to remember and cry with and get sympathetic phone calls, cards, hugs, and visits. I had no one who was talking.

I wanted my sister or my son. I was there for a couple of years, allowing my sister to talk and vent while bringing all the drama to my peaceful home. Now, she wasn't talking to me and refused to give me support in return.

I called my son the night before and asked if he would like to go with us to the service. He had already taken himself and his family away from the drama. He said," No way!"

I understood and respected his decision, but needed him to be at my side more than ever. He would have quietly supported me through that very tough time. He was so good at emotional support, but he had his own family to protect from all this dysfunction.

I felt like my world had ended.

Chapter 35

Life was very quiet. My son kept the kids away for a week while I grieved. I was broken and alone and didn't want to be away from my grandkids for too long. They were like taking vitamins! They were great infusions of love.

I spent that week feeling sad and alone and regretted speaking out at my dad's service. I wrote my mother, two brothers, and sister a letter of apology for my outburst. I even wrote an apology to my two male cousins on Facebook Messenger. I told them I was wrong and begged them all to forgive me. I felt like the biggest failure in the history of the world.

I remembered back to the night my father called me, and we rushed to his bedside. As we were leaving, my mother said that it was up to us four to plan his funeral. My three siblings and I were on her porch for a rare time together. I'm sure, as a mother, she would want nothing more than to see her four kids work together, but their control had already blinded her.

For a brief ten minutes—or so I thought— it was safe to suggest buying him a service at a funeral home and seeing the plot with my brother and sister. There was always so much double-sided talk in my family, and you could never believe what was being said.

I knew she was trying to include me, but it was too late. They didn't want me there. My heart broke for my mother; she had been married to him for sixty-six years and been by his side through it all. She worked tirelessly and never faltered in her devotion and love for him. She, indeed, was the greatest caregiver he could have had. I wanted to hold her and let her know how much I loved her and would be there to help her after he was gone. It could never happen; my brothers had taken over, and there was no coming back for her; she was under their spell.

A couple of my husband's co-workers sent me a plant, which meant everything to me. It's incredible how much support helps people.

But where were all the phone calls, cards, and support when someone died? I had never felt so alone. People always say, "Call me if you need anything," but when you are in a state of grief, it's hard to reach out and call someone.

As I was going to see my father on the last visit, I called my aunt, who lived in Oklahoma City. She said if there is anything that she can do, contact her. I said, "There is something you can do."

Her reaction told me she didn't expect it to be so soon.

"Would you feed my family after the service? They will need a place to gather and eat, and that would mean everything to me."

She sounded slightly offended when I asked but answered, "Of course I will." According to my mother, she fed them a very nice meal that evening after they returned.

I also told my aunt that I was walking through a tough time alone. I needed some support, and if she could ask some of the relatives to reach out to me, it would mean a lot. Again, she seemed offended that I would ask something like that. The problem was she and her family were already sitting in judgment towards me.

It would be easy later on to know who I no longer needed to keep in my life. None of them showed up for me, but I was so glad they showed up for my family. It definitely made a difference for them.

I read and reread the book of Job from the Bible that week. I felt like I was living a bit of his story. My phone buzzed one day; it was the relative who had slept with my ex-husband, aka one of Job's friends. There was no "I'm sorry for your loss conversation," she went right into judgment.

She began to tell me how God had told her to call me and how awful I was for treating my family that way at the cemetery. She wasn't there, by the way. She said, "I hope you have asked God to forgive you."

I stopped her and told her she was repeating gossip, which was none of her business. She kept trying to express her self-righteous attitude toward me, so I hung up. She wasn't worth the energy to listen to rude absurdities that were none of her business.

I didn't need another person to tell me what God wanted! I'd had a direct line to him for years. I knew she would be the last person He would send to me if I weren't listening to Him!

A call that could have been made in love and made a difference was a call made in judgment. I wouldn't be entertaining those calls. I had enough of my own self-judgment I was trying to process. You never know what another soul is going through; reaching out in love is one of our jobs as humans. We are here to share love and comfort, peace and joy. Sitting in judgment toward another creates barriers that love can't penetrate. Why are people so quick to judge, and why do we refuse to grow and learn?

Growing is painful, and no one wants to feel like a failure. It feels so much better to point fingers and talk about someone else than to look within and make a change. The only way for change to come is to look inside yourself and figure out why. I have been doing that my whole life. It makes other people uncomfortable, and they don't know how to handle such honesty.

They call me a troublemaker because I speak the truth and demand growth from those closest to me. I was sitting alone in my grief all because I spoke out and refused to be silent anymore on an abuse I had suffered and carried for years. That abuse had stolen my voice. It also stole my sense of worth.

I grew up thinking sex was love. My body and desires didn't matter; all that mattered was keeping a man happy. For most of my life, I felt my job was lying down and spreading my legs. It took years to learn that my feelings mattered, and I will always be a student in that regard.

I now have no regrets about speaking out at my father's "service." I had been abused and ridiculed over a critical issue between my father and me.

My father and I had made peace with it, which caused discomfort to those who had already formed their judgments against me. Their discomfort was none of my business at this point. My soul cried out at the cemetery, and that set me free!

My father truly loved me; I loved him and was his firstborn child. My blood was just as red as theirs was; my heart continued to beat in my chest, and I was still alive! I no longer needed their forgiveness or approval. I had stood up for the most important person in my world, me!

I had been worrying about all the wrong things. I was asking people who couldn't care less about me to forgive me for reacting to the horrible way they had treated me and left me out! I was lying down again and letting people take what they needed from me. I was automatically judged and outed because now they could look good, and no one would see their flaws if they pointed fingers at me.

Jesus said, "Why do you complain about the beam in your brother's eye when you clearly have a plank in your own eye!"

I didn't need to feel bad that these people were uncomfortable with my outburst. I needed to feel bad for myself. No one cared about my soul. They only cared about my bad behavior. I was the only one who could care for my soul and would not default on that job.

I now believed that I MATTERED!

Chapter 36

My son has been getting quieter since we moved to Texas in 2014.

We used to talk on the phone almost every day. While I noticed all the subtle changes, I never said anything. I knew if he could, he would tell me why. I felt he was doing his best to navigate his marriage. I could tell his wife felt threatened by our once very close relationship. I read his body language and saw him pulling back from me.

Throughout the years, he would tell me from time to time how much he appreciated me and never wanted me to feel used. I knew he was trying to tell me something was brewing, but he wouldn't talk about it due to his deep loyalty to his wife.

I never pressured him because I heard what he wasn't saying out loud, and I respected that. I honored their marriage and wanted them to be happy. I loved my daughter-in-law deeply.

I have always been a people watcher and read body language very well. I was reading her body language also.

She seemed uncomfortable with my son and I being close. She appeared uncomfortable that my grandchildren never wanted to go home. I tried to be sensitive to these issues. I wasn't trying to take anyone from her. I was loving on purpose with unconditional love. My grandchildren saw that, and it made them feel valued. Everyone needs that.

I'm glad I lived in the present moment with each of them. I had no idea our relationship would be shortened. And I had no idea I would finally lose my son. I had fought so hard for him throughout his life.

The truth was, he wasn't mine anymore, but hers. I didn't resent that. I just missed him. I missed his phone calls just to say hi.

From a young child throughout adulthood, when he would call me, he would say, "Hello Mom, this is (and say his name)." It was so endearing and always made me smile. I never received a call when he didn't say that.

I think I started reading body language because I grew up in a home where you couldn't freely express your concerns. I've studied what people weren't saying for years.

Sadly, my daughter-in-law's body language exuded jealousy and fear towards me and my daughter. She and my daughter never hit it off and never developed a relationship. My daughter loved her brother so much throughout life, but when he got married, all I ever heard from him was that it was my daughter's fault. I tried to bridge everyone, but my daughter lost the battle, fitting in with them. We were all walking on eggshells again.

I didn't take it personally that my daughter-in-law started showing up instead of him. I tried to involve her more in my conversations with him. She was very helpful to me after my dad died and dropped everything to come to me when I was having a panic attack. She did show up for me over the years.

I regret that we weren't able to communicate with each other when we needed to the most. I constantly pray for another chance to reconcile our lives together, and I hope we can do so someday. If we do, I will be different and bring my own boundaries and rules.

I love them all deeply. Maybe we weren't meant to have a whole lifetime. Maybe I have looked at it wrong since I was reading body language. I felt like something had shifted, and no one was talking.

My sister may have been stirring the pot out of her own jealousy over my close relationship with my family in Texas and my husband.

2019 was the first time we weren't invited to my son's house for Christmas Eve. We always had a party with finger foods and shared a good time together. It has become our tradition. I would read all the kids a story and let them open a gift from us. One of my son's lifelong friends and his family were always there. My granddaughter once told me it was her favorite day of the year. She loved it when we would come over; all the kids did.

I never realized how losing a parent affected you. It was as though I lost my identity. I was lucky enough to know him for sixty-three years. We had our issues from time to time, but I always knew my dad loved me. Sometimes, he acted like he didn't, but I knew in my soul he did.

For months, life was so different. I was struggling. I was struggling to find where I fit into life's circle. So many had judged me, and I felt my son and daughter-in-law were, too.

My sister had started talking to my daughter-in-law, and when I first noticed it, I thought it was great. I saw a change in my daughter-in-law and son's attitudes and felt my sister was stirring up trouble. I remembered she had expressed that she wanted my life.

Three times throughout the five years I took care of the grandkids, I received no notice that they would attend daycare the following Monday. Like I said earlier, I had the kids from 6:30 a.m. to 6:30 p.m. every day for years.

I had my house set up for the children. I had one room with twin beds, play areas, books, and teaching materials. My backyard was a playground any kid would treasure. It always had a playhouse, trampoline, roller coaster, and toys to play with all day. My home and energy were dedicated to helping raise them. I loved it and cherished the fact that I could be there to enjoy all four of them. I woke up at 5:00 a.m. to have my alone time and get myself ready for their energy. We had a schedule, and I kept it and looked forward to it.

I kept the two youngest boys from infants until around two years old. They put them in daycare after that, and I would get them after school a lot. Most of the kids always spent the weekend with us, too. I never received the proper respect of being informed beforehand that there would be a change. It made me feel like my time didn't count, my sleep didn't matter, and my energy towards them wasn't seen.

It devastated me when they would give me no notice.

I was in my 60s and smack dab in menopause with profuse sweating all the time. I was tired. I would have welcomed a break if they had respected me enough to tell me beforehand. Instead, I used each break to cry and rebuild myself.

As I look back, my heart problems were probably from all the stress of my parents when I had the heart attack. I went from one stressful situation with them to a physically exhausting situation where I felt no respect from my son and daughter-in-law. I was performing according to someone else's rules and still jumping through hoops to keep others happy.

Chapter 37

The end of April 2020 brought its own stresses along with the coronavirus. I had an argument with my daughter-in-law about not giving me notice that the kids would be returning to school again. I was tired of being left out when I was doing so much work. I asked her to respect my energy and time. My daughter-in-law refused to have a conversation with me.

I knocked on her door and tried to have a conversation about it. There was no remorse or desire to reconcile. Her only response was, "Debbie, I feel like you are expecting an apology from me, and it's just not coming."

At that point, I lost my temper with her. I felt disrespected and called her a bad name as I peeled out of her neighborhood and yelled at her.

Since my father's death and being around so much finger-pointing and blame, I felt very alone in the world and really would have benefited from having a good heart-to-heart with her and my son. We needed to have a conversation about their lack of respect towards me.

For over fourteen years, I had a long list of things I could say and not say in their world. I was told how to dress, talk, laugh, and act. As long as I was willing to perform without complaint or have my own rules, they were content to use me, and I was welcome to join their world.

When I spoke out, they arrogantly ignored my pleas and requests. Their silence was manipulation. Removing my grandchildren from our lives was also manipulation. I did not matter to them when I was noisy. I could be in their world if I obeyed their rules and kept my mouth shut.

The one thing I know about them is they would protect their children and relationships first. They would have kept them away if they felt I was not good for their kids. They must have been fed some information that sounded close to the truth. I felt my sister was probably involved.

I apologized for losing my temper via text and begged for a resolution. But no one would talk to me.

I left birthday gifts for the kids on their porch. I later received a text telling me not to put any gifts on the porch for birthdays or Christmas, and no mail, emails, texts, or phone calls. They wanted space.

So far, we have had four years of silence with no attempt to reconcile. I have never been more devastated or broken. I sobbed every single day for three years straight. This was the greatest loss of my life.

I didn't know how to navigate life without my son or his children. I didn't even want to learn how to. He had been my one constant in life, and I always knew he'd be there. I watched for his car every day to pull into my driveway for three years.

I became a hermit. I slept and cried and prayed for his return. I stopped leaving the house.

I stopped going anywhere I thought I could run into them. I didn't want my grandkids to see me and wonder why they couldn't talk to me. They were devastated by this, too. We loved each other so very much. My broken heart was for them. How would they be able to process losing unconditional love?

I was devastated over them learning that when someone you love so much makes a mistake, it's okay to throw them away. I realize these were not my lessons to teach. I had taught them all the lessons God had allowed me. My time was done. They were my grandchildren, and their parents wanted them to learn different lessons I couldn't teach them.

I had done my job.

They both love their four children deeply, and I knew my grandchildren would always be in good hands with them. I was only lent a small time with them and will treasure it forever. They will always be my dear grandchildren whom I love beyond words. There will be a spot for them in my life as long as my heart beats.

For now, mom and dad have lessons to teach them that they need to learn. That's how it's supposed to be. I'm not angry anymore; I'm only sad. I will always be sad at the loss of their presence in my life. There isn't a day, not one, that I don't think of all of them and miss them.

I still can't do some things because of my memories. I am thankful I had the time, but my heart will always be looking for them. I pray they will always feel the deep love my husband, me, and their aunt carry for them forever. My prayers will never cease for them.

What about the lesson of forgiveness? It wasn't my lesson to teach. I had been removed, and I think it was supposed to be that way for now.

Chapter 38

I was talking to my mother one day, and she told me my sister had told my daughter-in-law that she highly suggested she keep her children away from me.

It began to make sense that my sister had gotten into my daughter-in-law's head.

Toward the end of May 2020, I asked my daughter to go to Sedona, Arizona, with me. I wanted to sit alone with God on the mountains and get some hope back in my heart. I didn't want to live anymore. I prayed God would take me. I begged Him. I had never been this desolate. It was truly the darkest time of my life.

I missed my sister, so I called and asked if she would like to join us in Sedona. She was mad at me for losing it at my father's service and told me so.

I told her I had been deleted from my son's and grandkids' lives and needed some support. I told her I was a mess because I miss my grandchildren. Everything reminded me of them.

She was low on money. I told her I would give her the money if she wanted to go with us, and she quickly agreed. Clearly, I was buying her time, love, and support. I would realize it even more very soon.

I warned her I would be crying a lot. I hadn't stopped in the last two months. I hoped to find some solace and peace while sitting on top of the great red mountains in Sedona.

As I drove, I cried and prayed out loud in spurts. I occasionally looked in my rearview mirror and would catch a glimpse of my sister looking at me like I was crazy. I could tell she was judging me, and I began to regret bringing her. She showed no understanding of my tears and deep grief. My tears gave no notice, and memories flooded my soul.

Maybe I was crazy; I had lost everyone and everything and was just trying to navigate life one day at a time. I continued to listen to the voice that has never led me astray. I knew I just needed to sit in God's presence, and I had heard Sedona was a good place to do that.

It was a great place just to sit and be with God. As I sat on top of the smallest mountain we could climb, I reveled in God's presence. I closed my eyes and folded my hands in prayer, felt the wonderful hot rays from the sun, and let the tears flow from my eyes as I remembered and regained my strength.

I wanted to sit for hours and could have. It was a holy place. I felt like it was sacred ground and treated it that way. Everyone who walked up did the same.

My sister didn't. She talked out loud to everyone who came up. It felt like she was trying to disturb me and didn't want me to do what I was doing. One time, I "shushed" her, and she gave me a dirty look.

I began to find her irritating and just tried to let her and my daughter hang out. She wanted to shop, and I wanted to pray. She was a big distraction and did not help me feel safe to express my feelings.

I took what I could from God the time we were there. We had decided to go to Las Vegas, where my sister's sons lived. It seemed the closer we got to Vegas, the more hyper her spirit became. She was on my last nerve. Undoubtedly, she wasn't my friend anymore. She seemed to do everything possible to irritate me with her judgmental spirit.

By the time we arrived at our room in Las Vegas, I needed some space from her. I went to my room, closed the door, and began to journal and pray for strength. I wished I had not invited her. She was not helpful but selfish.

I came out crying and told her and my daughter I couldn't handle it. All I could think about was my son and his family, and I wasn't handling this loss well at all. This was my worst loss. I was so upset.

She raised her voice at me and sternly said, "Debbie, what do you want from me right now?"

I said, "SUPPORT. LOVE. UNDERSTANDING and HOPE! I don't want to live without my son in my life."

She started telling me about her suicide attempt, which I have heard a million times, and how she understood my feelings.

"I'm not suicidal! I just don't want to be here without my son! I don't know how!"

She kept trying to tell me how I was feeling, and I yelled at her to stop it! I told her I couldn't hear anyone else's sad story. I didn't have enough room in my soul for anything else. I just wanted to be heard and comforted.

The end result was the next morning, and she told me I had brought her cancer back by screaming at her. I was a very selfish woman, and it's no wonder my son had left. She said she had been bleeding all night, and it was all my fault. She then told me she wouldn't be riding back to Oklahoma with me. She would stay in Vegas, and her sons would take her back.

I said, "That's your choice, but I didn't bring you out here to leave you."

She said she didn't feel safe with me. I had given her my credit card a few months earlier to pay all her utilities. I then told her if she didn't feel safe with me, it wouldn't make sense for her to continue to use my credit card. I would be canceling it immediately. She began to scream about how selfish I was and how I could leave her boys in darkness and with no water!

"I'm not doing that; you are." I canceled my card immediately, and my daughter and I went to California to see the ocean.

My daughter and I took our time sightseeing and driving back to Texas. I didn't feel much better because of the negativity from my sister. Each day continued to be a deep struggle for me. I had no idea how to begin to navigate life without my son or grandchildren.

I had been with them all over the Dallas area over the years. I couldn't turn a corner without memories of our time together flooding my soul. I couldn't quit crying.

Their bedroom was still set up. I kept the door closed. The backyard was full of playground equipment! I had nowhere to go without the memories being in my face. There wasn't a room in my home that didn't exude their energy.

I was completely devastated.

In June, I called a resort in Sedona and signed up for some healing classes for a week. I asked my husband to go; he could work from the room while I was in class, and we could hike and pray afterward.

We spent a week there, and it was very helpful. I met some very good people who led me to the path of hope again. They taught me some new tools, and my husband and I sat with God every day on the smallest vortex.

We both saw visions in the great mountains and received great strength, being so much closer to Heaven on the mountaintop. God helped us regain strength and courage to face life some more.

I had texted my sister, trying to make amends during our time in Sedona. I told her I loved her and hoped she was feeling better. When she heard I was there with my husband, she began to write a long letter, texting how awful I was.

She brought up his infidelity and asked how I could possibly forgive him! I told her my marriage was none of her business and to stay out of it.

She started insulting me in the most intimate ways. She was trying to keep me from growing and was evidently jealous that I had brought my husband there. Why would that bother her? Because I was living her life?

She even said, "Do you know when your son was three, he used to call me mommy?"

I replied, "You think that had anything to do with the fact that we all lived in the same house for five years since his birth? What's your point? Am I supposed to be offended by that?"

I could see she only wanted to fight and throw boulders, so I blocked and deleted her texts immediately. If I continued to allow such horrible and hateful accusations to enter my mind, I would never grow.

That was the beginning of choosing who I no longer needed in my life's circle. I deleted her and every extended family member who had been quietly watching all the drama unfold while not lending support.

I would no longer allow judges, prosecutors, stone throwers, or peeping toms in my life anymore. I was taking charge, and my life was my business. I was the CEO!

My tribe got down to three: my husband, daughter, and I.

I am not leaving my kids out with my husband, but at the time of this great loss, they were over a thousand miles away and didn't stay in touch. I was incapable of reaching out to anyone for three long years.

My husband's son began coming for a week to spend Christmas with us in 2021. I loved it! I now look forward to that time each year. His visits helped bring rays of light back into my heart.

Chapter 39

Getting back to Texas after our trip to Sedona in June was helpful. When I would venture outside, the little neighborhood girls would always say hello. They were absolutely beautiful, very sweet, and kind.

The youngest was the same age as my youngest grandson. Every time I talked to her, I saw him. She looked a lot like him and made some of the same faces. I would go inside and cry for hours after talking to them.

It was hard. I didn't want to hurt the girls, but it hurt me so much to be around them. There was also a precious boy named Solomon across the street who frequently talked to me.

My heart was so very fragile. I can now see that God had sent them to help me heal. They were the first ones He sent, and there would be many more!

They kept coming back, and I'd let them come inside to play with a huge doll house I had decorated. They would spend forever in there if I'd let them. I could only handle an hour at a time, and it triggered so many memories as I watched them be normal, beautiful children playing just like my grandkids did.

They wanted to call me grandma, but it hurt too much! I loved them, but my heart had a lot of healing to do. They tried calling me Aunt Debbie for a while. I guess my calling wasn't just for my own grandchildren. These girls were precious, and I loved them. They would visit almost every day. I still kept the bedroom door closed to my grandkids' room. It was still holy ground to me.

My husband, daughter, and our two dogs went with me to Sedona again in August 2020. We stayed for two weeks on top of the mountain with breathtaking views. We sat in God's presence for hours, bathing in the heat of the sun and beauty. It was another empowering trip, helping each of us to grow. We hiked and sat with God. It felt so good just to sit and simply be with Him. My husband and I have a very strong spiritual connection, and I love that we can share God's presence with each other.

Before we left for Sedona in August, we had to put another one of the four dogs to sleep. Her name was Tia Maria. She had been one of my son and daughter-in-law's dogs. She was aggressive when my daughter-in-law was pregnant, and they feared she would bite the babies. I took her and two others that they had at the time.

She was a feisty five-pound black chihuahua with a bit of white and gold fur around her head. She fit in well with our pack, and we loved her!

She was seventeen years old when she died, and it crushed us all. My daughter called herself Tia's mother. It was yet another loss and someone to mourn. I'm always amazed at how much energy a soul takes up. The void left from her five pounds was shocking. It was like a huge mountain had been removed from our presence. Her life was meaningful and impactful to us all. Her weight did not match the power of her spirit!

Taking three trips that summer to Sedona was healing and helpful. It helped me see that I could still wake up each day and live life, however sad my heart was. It would take years to get my heart in a place of real hope again. I was in uncharted territory in my life. I had never had this much time alone to process.

Maybe my son and daughter-in-law gave me a gift I had never been given in my life: time. I now had all the time I needed to feel and heal from a hectic, traumatic life with no interruptions.

I began to dig in the dirt in my backyard. I wanted to create a serene setting like I had seen in the Botanical Gardens in Fort Worth, Texas. I started to build structures out of bamboo fencing and zip ties. The 2021 freeze killed our two large and beautiful shade trees in our backyard, and we had them removed. We had no shade, so I began building and digging from scratch.

I first had to get rid of the huge trampoline, roller coaster, play house, and toys. It was 2022, and we still hadn't heard from my son. This was my first step in letting go. If I didn't let go, there would be no room to grow. It was hard, but step by step, I began to grow.

I have added more structures each year and now have a beautiful, serene garden to enjoy. It is a peaceful place full of greenery, statues, water sounds, birds singing, chimes, and the neighbor's trees talking as the wind rustles their great branches and leaves.

Digging in the dirt is very therapeutic and has helped me. My tears water the beauty as I cry into the soil, and new growth is seen physically and emotionally. God knew how very low I was and how unloved I felt after the trouble with my family and then my son.

I felt like the most unlovable human alive. I had failed at life.

I had lost my entire family, but most of all, my dear firstborn child.

I needed love but didn't know if I would ever feel loved again. I was at the lowest depths I had ever been. I would pray constantly, and God began to send me miracles!

One morning, I was digging to make a new walkway. I had made one the day before and poured a few more rocks into it. I looked down on the first large rock to notice that a heart had been carved into the stone overnight. I stared in disbelief! Wow, God gave me my first heart, showing me I was loved! I ran and brought my husband out to show him. He was amazed, too. It's still there, and every time I walk by it, I am reminded of the first time God threw me a heart from Heaven.

For a solid year, everywhere I went, I would see hearts. The sky would be full of them. I don't mean one; I mean a sky full of heart clouds as far as you could see. He was trying to tell me He loved me and could see me, and I was not forgotten!

He even went so far as to create a heart spot on my arm overnight. I woke up, looked at my right forearm, and saw a perfect heart that had not been there before. I showed my dermatologist and she says it's perfectly healthy, with no sign of skin cancer. I have found so many things in the shape of hearts over the last three years that remind me that I am loved, worthy, and seen!

I have tried to stay in touch with my mother so many times. Every time I would see her, though, I would be reminded by her how much my brothers hated me and how they would never forgive me. I would leave each time feeling more defeated and unloved. I was tired of hearing it and tired of being reminded what a horrible human they thought I was.

One day, I stopped her and said, "Now tell me again, why do I need their forgiveness?"

"Oh, Debbie, you know what you did was terrible at your daddy's service."

"Oh, was it? Please tell my brothers the next time you see them and they start talking about me that I no longer need their forgiveness," I told her, continuing, "Please ask them to stop throwing stones and perhaps work on getting the plank out of their own eyes. I don't remember ever hearing them say, 'I'm sorry' for their bad behaviors toward me!"

I woke up one morning and felt strongly that my aunt had died. This was the aunt that I would spend my summers with each year. She was like a second mother to me. I googled her name and found her obituary. I was shocked when I read that she had died a year ago. I immediately texted my mother and asked her if she knew her sister had died. She said yes.

My mother told me that my older brother and the aunt who fixed them dinner after my father's service had decided not to inform me. My brother had told them he would not be showing up if I came. I was really shocked that they would be so childish and judgmental toward something they had only heard about.

I wrote all four of my cousins a letter telling them I had just found out by googling their mother's name and that she was dead. I sent them my love and sympathies. Then, I removed their numbers from my contacts and blocked them. I did the same with my aunt. These were unkind and judgmental people who would never get to sit at my table again!

I had a decision to make. Do I keep allowing myself to be beaten up or remove myself from the toxicity? I've chosen to remove myself from the toxicity of their lives.

Chapter 40

In May 2022, I decided to get away and be alone for a week. I couldn't stop crying, and I missed my grandchildren so very badly. I was craving time to be in a secluded place where I could get up at all hours and pray, write, cry, and feel without being disturbed. I got a room in another town and spent a week staring out the window at a serene setting of wild animals.

On my way to this room, I noticed a woman walking with a cane as I got off the interstate. I never picked people up, but I was very drawn to this lady. I turned around and went to her and asked if she needed help. She was well dressed, carried a nice purse, striking deep blue eyes, and had a limp. She said she needed a ride to a certain place, and I took her.

During our ride, I felt she was no ordinary woman; something was different. Her eyes reminded me of my favorite cousin. She kept saying how much my laugh sounded just like her grandma's. She said my voice did, too. She was about my age. I thought, "Great. Grief must have aged me. I must look old!"

She talked about how I reminded her of her grandma the whole ride. I dropped her off and stared at her as she walked away. I felt like she may have been an angel and was reminding me I was still a grandma and that I still mattered.

I spent the week praying and journaling. It was a good week to sit with God. By the end of the week, my daughter called me to wish me a Happy Mother's Day. She asked when I was coming back, and I said I didn't know. I'm getting a lot out of being alone and praying. I said, "Why don't you drive here tomorrow, and we'll go out for lunch." She did, and we went to Applebee's.

We had gotten our food, and I was just about to take a bite when I felt arms wrap around me, and a girl said, "Hello Grandma, how are you? I've missed you so much!" I let out a little screech and instinctively hugged the child back!

We embraced for a solid minute, and it felt so good! She looked me in the eyes and said, "Oh. I thought you were my grandma; you look just like her."

I said, "Honey, you look just like my beautiful granddaughter, too. Maybe God created this moment for both of us," as I wiped a tear away.

She nodded her head yes. It was another angelic encounter. One that I really needed.

The next day, I went into a Ross store. Out of the corner of my eyes, I saw a very tall man, about seven feet tall. He wore a nice suit and had dark hair and piercing brown eyes. I turned around to get a better look because he was extraordinarily beautiful. He had disappeared! He was so tall he couldn't hide anywhere. I looked everywhere in the store, and he was gone in a second.

Later in the month, my daughter and I were walking into an Olive Garden in Dallas, and I saw him again! Before I could tell her to look at him, he had disappeared. I felt God had sent angels down to Earth to look after me and let me know I was loved since humans had failed me.

My husband, daughter, and I went to Telluride, Colorado, a year ago. We were walking the streets of one of the small towns nearby. We passed a very eccentric-looking man wearing a safari uniform and thick, round glasses. As we passed him, I made eye contact with him.

He yelled out, "Young lady, God is watching you. God is watching you!"

I raised my hand in acknowledgment and said, "Thank you."

As I turned, I saw another beautiful, tall man standing nearby who exuded peace and smiled at me. I recognized these as angelic encounters from God to let me know I am seen, loved, and not forgotten.

As the holidays rolled around in 2021, I felt like everyone probably needed human contact as much as I did after being in isolation from the virus, so I created a Friendsgiving event for all those on my street. We have a large street with about sixty houses.

I made a flier, and my husband and I passed it out to every house. It said, "If you need a friend or company or just want to get around others, bring a dish, and let's get together."

We provided the meat and drinks, and they were to bring anything else. I invited the fire department, and we had over a hundred people.

I was outside one day preparing my yard for the event, and my young friend Solomon came up to me and said, "Mrs. Debbie, I won't be able to attend your event, and I'm sad."

I said, "Why not?"

"Because I am Muslim and don't eat pork."

"Well, do you eat chicken?"

"Yes!"

I told him we would put the pork on a separate table. I also told him it was okay that he was Muslim. He smiled and said, "Thank you. I'll tell my mom!"

He had become my friend. He loved to stop by after school a few times a week and just chat for about ten minutes. He was so sweet, kind, and loving. I kept Hot Wheels and Nerf stuff in my closet for him, and he would choose a toy before he left each time.

His mother told me one day that she had told him not to bother us so much. He said, "Oh, Mom, I'm not bothering them. They need me!"

Only God knew how very true that was and how much it helped to be loved by these children at such a dark time in my life.

We had a wonderful time at the Friendsgiving event. It was so good just to laugh and talk with other people again.

Solomon's mom had just had a baby boy a couple of weeks before, and her mother was here from Saudi Arabia to help. She brought out her coffee pot and taught us the proper way to drink Saudi coffee. We all laughed and loved talking with her as she took pictures with her new American friends!

I have found that the fastest way to get out of being sad and take your power back is to reach out to someone else.

Do something good for someone.

Call someone.

Help them when they are struggling.

Sitting around feeling sorry for yourself keeps you in victim mode, and no one wants to be around a constant victim.

No one can change the world you live in like you can. Take a chance—chances open doors.

My little friend continued to visit me, as did the girls.

One morning, about 7:30 a.m., he came over crying as he rang the doorbell. My husband answered the door as Solomon quickly said, "I need to talk to Mrs. Debbie now."

"She's asleep", my husband said.

I heard him from the door, grabbed a robe, and ran to his panicked voice. "What's going on, Solomon?"

"We're moving to Australia, and I came to say goodbye."

"What? When? "I asked.

"In thirty minutes," he cried.

I hugged him, gave him a Hot Wheel, and told him how much I would miss him. I then took the dog they had given us over to say goodbye to the family. It was a sad day. I could see Solomon was heartbroken. He was a good boy, and I do miss him. I see him as an angel.

The dog they gave us was his, and he was heartbroken to get rid of him. They couldn't take him to Australia, so they asked if I would take him. I promised them he would have a good home. His name was Rocco, and he was a very sweet Pomeranian.

His mother introduced me to her friend as I was saying goodbye to them. She was there helping them get their house in order. I started helping her finish closing up their house, and we became fast friends.

That's how God sent the next angels into my life.

He was pulling angels out of Heaven, sending children over, sending people from Saudi Arabia, and now He had sent me a Pakistani woman who became my new best friend.

After I cleaned up my tribe and got rid of those who no longer belonged, God started fresh by sending me pure love. We grew to love each other quickly because we are so much alike and have so much in common. There's no need for lengthy explanations; we know each other on a soul level.

We have common hobbies and laugh a lot. When my Sana tells me she loves me, I believe her because she means it, and I feel it. It is God-like love. There is no ulterior motive from either of us. It is pure friendship dropped out of Heaven, just like the angels were.

I eat Halal food each time we are together, and it's delicious! We celebrate special days together. We are the same!

Her husband is wonderful, too. They have two sons, whom I have grown very close to. They are about the same age as my two youngest grandsons. I have fallen in love with them. They begged to come to my house just like my grandkids did. I have come to accept that I have the gift of being a grandmother, and it would be selfish not to share it with so many who need it.

The boys and I sit and talk a lot. We watch movies, and they love to help me create and add more beauty to the gardens.

One of the other dogs I had taken from my son was a beautiful black Pomeranian named Harley. He had a very sweet, quiet, loving, and wise spirit. In 2023, at the age of seventeen, he fell off the bed while asleep and injured his neck. He had a previous back and neck injury from being hit by a car in 2011. The vet had told me any fall in his life would likely paralyze him.

He didn't recover and died from his injuries. We were once again entirely heartbroken. My friend told her boys that Harley had died, and immediately, the younger one said, "Oh, Mommy, I want to go to Harley's funeral."

After I got his ashes back, they came over, and we held a funeral for him.

The younger one said, "I'll carry the cross!" He looked around the gardens and found one. The older one had the box of ashes.

We formed a procession, and I led the way to an area I had built as a memory garden for the animals. They followed behind me, holding the ashes and the cross, my daughter behind the cross-bearer, and my friend followed her.

We laid the cross and Harley in the designated spot, and I told them about some great memories of Harley. I allowed each person to share something about him, too. Then I said a prayer as we all held our hands open to God.

As I ended, my dear Sana said, "May God's blessing and peace be with him," in Arabic.

We all said Amen together.

It was one of the most beautiful sights I have ever witnessed.

One God heard the prayers being prayed from the heart, from two perspectives that day, and His face was shining down in favor of us all.

No one needed to announce their choice of religion; it was absolutely irrelevant. God was present with no rules or walls, as we all respected each other's differences in pure love.

God loves us all.

He placed a very white grandma with two Pakistani boys; we are like family. The love is real. I'm very grateful. I teach them, and they teach me. We have fun, and God shines His love and light upon us all.

My friend's sister came to visit last summer from Canada. She brought with her two very handsome boys, eight and three years old. When they came to my house, I greeted them, and the three-year-old fell asleep during the walk through the gardens. They left, and he woke up at their house. He was crying and saying he wanted to go back to grandma's house! So that added two more beautiful souls to the list.

Chapter 41

I embraced the people God was sending my way the best I could and appreciated the refreshing way they loved me. The truth is each child I received into my life reminded me of my profound loss, and I saw my four grandchildren in their eyes.

There were triggers everywhere I turned. My home was saturated with their spirit. Their magic marker writings were still on my walls; I couldn't bear to erase them. For four years, there was not one day that my soul was not thinking of my dear son and grandchildren. My grief was unbearable, and I cried daily.

I told Dean we needed to get out of there. We agreed that moving away from daily and constant triggers would help us heal.

I began to search for a new place for us to move. I looked all over the United States, anywhere we had vacationed, and loved places where his family lived and any beautiful, serene setting I could find. My search went on for four years. Nothing ever popped up that we both loved, and there were always reasons we didn't want to move there.

One day, Dean and I sat down and had a conversation about the move. I don't know why, but up until now, we have not made a list of desires and needs. There were a couple of things we had to have, and one was a VA Center and the other a military base. That helped narrow our search down.

That very night, I was searching online and found a house that had just been placed on the market earlier in the day. I looked at it, got excited, and ran to Dean to show him. His reaction was out of the norm for him, and he said it has everything we have asked for and more! I love it! I immediately texted an old friend who I knew had a son who was a realtor. She connected us, and we went with a checkbook in hand to purchase the house a day later. We had already made our minds up; God had sent us towards our next move in life!

Again, just like all my other lists in life, we got exactly what we asked for and so much more! We began to prepare for our exit from Trophy Club. We hired an excellent realtor and prepared our house for sale.

We wrote another letter to God, which said: "Thank you, God, for a speedy sale and a bidding war to get the best price for our home." We placed the note and a St. Joseph medal in a baggy and buried it in the front yard.

The day our house went on the market, we sold it to a cash buyer. God had not forgotten us and was still leading us even though our world was so very dark with grief. It would be a while before we could reminisce about all the fun and precious times we had with the kids. At the time, it was just too painful to talk about.

I had written a chapter in another book called Courage Under Siege, Volume 7, and needed to create a website in late spring. Quite often, I have quoted Robert Frost's poem, which talks about taking the road not taken in life.

I have always been a leader and have created my own road many times when I wasn't satisfied with the status quo. I refuse to follow the crowd and will, quite often, be found alone on my own road, paving the way for someone else. It made sense to call my website https://RoadNotTaken.net, which was created in late spring of 2024.

Dean and I closed and moved into our new house in July 2024 on a street called Road Not Taken! It was another heart thrown from Heaven and the Creator who reminded us that He was still watching and leading us. We were not forgotten, and we were loved. We were brought to a serene and beautiful place to decompress and heal from the greatest loss and time of our lives!

For the past eight weeks, I have gotten up at 4:00 a.m. and sat under the stars and moon, staring at a beauty I hadn't enjoyed since I was a child.

I sit every morning staring at the Heavens and giving all my burdens, sadness, loss, love, and hopes to the one who needed no help creating Orion.

I stare at the constellations in the eastern sky as I decompress and come down from a very long life of constant grief and stress!

My strength comes from those skies, and I am learning to sit in peace for the first time in a long time.

God has taught me that He cares for me. I am learning what peace, serenity, and self-care look like for this next chapter of life.

It's been a long road.

Epilogue

Ecclesiastes 3:1-8, KJV

To everything there is a season and a time to every purpose under the heaven;

A time to be born, and a time to die; a time to plant, and a time to pluck up that which is planted;

A time to kill, and a time to heal; a time to break down, and a time to build up;

A time to weep, and a time to laugh; a time to mourn, and a time to dance;

A time to cast away stones, and a time to gather stones together; a time to embrace, and a time to refrain from embracing;

A time to get, and a time to lose; a time to keep, and a time to cast away;

A time to rend, and a time to sew; a time to keep silent, and a time to speak; a time to love, and a time to hate; a time of war, and a time of peace.

About the Author

Debbie Widhalm
debbiewidhalm48@gmail.com
https://roadnottaken.net

Debbie Widhalm personally knows deep pain, abuse, rejection, abandonment, the feeling of being unloved and unwanted, grief, and loss so well. She has channeled those feelings and made a choice to love on purpose in life, thus creating deep empathy for all mankind and creatures. Her career as a Burn Nurse for 20 years gave her plenty of opportunity to express this empathy. She continues to be a student in the study of death and dying and the afterlife. She holds a certificate as a Grief Recovery Specialist.

She loves to create beauty from ashes and has spent the last four years in her backyard digging in the dirt, creating a Zen oasis where you can feel God walking. During this time, as she walked through a time of unimaginable loss, Debbie planted bushes, trees, and flowers as well as built structures, while watering the beauty with her tears of grief. Her writings express her emotions well!

If you would like to read more of her writings, Debbie will have a children's book out in the Spring of 2025, called The Story of Tops the Chinese Goose. It's a wonderful story that teaches inclusion, love, and grief.

Be on the lookout as this author shares her work!

Made in the USA
Columbia, SC
28 January 2025